HEAVENLY STRATEGIES FOR VICTORY

Bongani Maluka

© Copyright 2026
ISBN: 978-1-0492-3301-7
EPUB: 978-1-0492-3302-4

TABLE OF CONTENTS

THANDI
SHILOH
DOMINGO

F

FOREWORD

For as long as I can remember, I wrestled with a kind of defeat that mocked my confession of Christian faith.

I loved God, at least as far as emotional love is concerned, I believed I sincerely loved Him. I prayed, I fasted, I served in church and even rose up the ranks of leadership, and yet the cycles of defeat, chaos and grappling with sin remained the same.

I could not understand why my Christian life bore the marks of witchcraft, timidity, stagnation, and constant limitation. Even more battling was the same cycles I was noticing in my life, were mirrored by those I served Christ with. It seemed like this life of defeat was normal. It was even justified in conversations that heralded our humanity over holiness. We wore the phrase "we're only human" like a pacifier that only served to satisfy us with defeat. I often wondered in silence what, then, did Jesus truly accomplish on the Cross if I could still live so defeated? What was the point of this man dying if I could justify lawlessness and mediocrity with simply being human?

5

Why did demonic torment still circle my mind and my dreams? Why was I breaking out in cold sweats in the middle of the night, screaming from nightmares which felt and presented themselves as real in my awake state? Furthermore, why were those who were ministering to me seeming not to have answers to my predicaments when I dared to ask? Why were breakthroughs always delayed or short-lived? Why did fear still have a voice in a life that was supposedly redeemed?

No one had ever told me that what my spirit received at salvation does not automatically translate into my soul. I certainly had heard that a human being is a tri-partite being comprising of the spirit, soul and body, however, the spirit and soul were sketchy definitions, whereas the body was a clearly defined matter I could touch and feel. I did not know that redemption must be enforced, not merely acknowledged. A will can exist for as long as one is alive, but can never be enforced whilst the principle is alive. But when the principle has died, the will can remain unenforced even though it is available to be enforced. This has been the life of many believers. No enforcement of a will and testament, largely due to limited knowledge on even knowing HOW TO enforce it. I discovered – painfully - that victory is not passive; it is stewarded.

The real turning point came when I began to understand the intersection of truths I had never fully encountered such as;
-   the fall of man and its legal implications,
-   God as Judge, Father and Friend, as well as His altar foundations which are JUSTICE and RIGHTEOUSNESS. My hyper introduction to God's love and Grace never allowed me to see Him as a Holy God who requires Holiness. As such my relationship with Him was a revolving door of

intentional sin knowing that I can go back to Him when I'm done indulging my sin and utter an apology which was never meaningful and reflected in the subsequent change of behavior

- Jesus as Mediator,
- His Blood as an eternal Witness,
- my obedience as a response to covenant,
- the finished works of Christ as a platform,
- intimacy with the Word and the Holy Spirit as empowerment,
- and the manifold wisdom of the Church as a spiritual ecosystem of authority.
- the clarity of the soul and how the light of God's Word should be executed to transform what the bible refers to as the mind/heart/soul.

This convergence opened my eyes to the authority of the believer—not as a theory, but as a lived reality. It was here that the torment broke, the cycles shattered, and the timidity dissolved. It was here that I stopped surviving and started standing.

I am beyond convinced that Heavenly Strategies for Victory is a book I needed, and that would have helped me to fast-track the revelation of my authority in Christ. It truly is an answered prayer as a tool of clarity, light and understanding to move believers from conversion to transformation. . My prayer is that as you read, the same revelation that lifted me from defeat into dominion will awaken in you, and you will finally see who you are, what you carry, and why hell fears the believer who understands their authority.

By Apostle Thandi Shiloh Domingo

NALEDI
MQABA

T

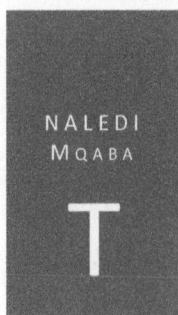

VICTORY TESTIMONY 1

For more than a decade, I lived in the shadows of mental health struggles - battling depression, anxiety, and surviving multiple suicide attempts. My pain began long before adulthood, shaped by witnessing my mother's own mental health challenges. For years, I believed healing was impossible, convinced that the best I could do was cope, manage triggers, and survive from one moment to the next.

But everything changed when I encountered God's grace and the guidance of my mentor. In 2021, I declared freedom over my life, holding onto Philippians 4:13: "I can do all things through Christ who strengthens me." I even marked that turning point with a semicolon tattoo - a symbol of survival, continuation, and hope. Yet life tested me once more when I faced sexual assault, a moment that threatened to undo all my progress. I felt shattered and unable to pray, but God surrounded me with people who stood in the gap when I had no strength left.

Through prayer, fasting, and mentorship, I discovered that my pain carried purpose. Today, I speak boldly about mental health and healing because I have lived that journey myself. I joined movements against gender-based violence, prayed for national change, and witnessed a miracle when GBV was declared a national disaster in South Africa. That moment reminded me that healing is not only possible for me - but for countless others.

My story is proof that no matter how dark life becomes, there is always hope. There is victory and comfort in God, and there is power in mentorship. I am living evidence that your story does not end with pain - your purpose truly begins there.

LEBOGANG
METSWI

T

VICTORY TESTIMONY 2

Today, I testify of the sovereignty and healing power of God. In 2021, I began losing weight rapidly, battling exhaustion and a loss of appetite. At first, I assumed it was end-of-year fatigue. But after several consultations, multiple sets of blood tests, and countless follow-ups, my doctor still could not find the cause. My weight dropped from 79kg to 58kg by early 2022. By May, I was sick almost every week and constantly placed on sick leave while the doctor searched for answers.

I will never forget the day she called urgently, insisting I return immediately. When I finally saw her, she looked at me with deep concern and handed me an admission letter. I had Bone TB - tuberculosis that had spread beyond the lungs to affect the bones, joints, and spine. And as if that was not enough my kidneys had collapsed, and she warned me that without urgent dialysis, I would die. Fear gripped me, yet I still refused hospitalization for days, praying and declaring healing. But my strength deteriorated until I could no longer stand. My family watched helplessly as I grew weaker, and I even prepared them for my death.

Eventually, I surrendered and went to the hospital alone, barely able to walk. I was admitted straight into high care, placed on drips, and monitored closely. My memory, speech, and orientation deteriorated. Specialists diagnosed multiple conditions and even warned my children to prepare for the worst. Yet prayers intensified. My family, my church leaders, and my sister-friend stood in the gap for me when I had no strength left.

On the third day, the dialysis machine that awaited me was removed. Slowly, I began to recover. After nearly three months in hospital and a second hospitalization, God restored my health, my mind, and my strength.

During this season, a song carried me - "Made a Way" by Travis Greene. Its message became my anthem: God made a way when there seemed to be none. Today, I am living proof that Jehovah Rapha still heals.

May this testimony give hope to the hopeless. May my testimony remind someone that He is still Jehovah Rapha - the God who heals. Amen.

PREFACE

P

PREFACE

For as long as I can remember, I have been captivated by the way God empowers ordinary men and women, like my wife's mentee (Testimony 1) and my mother-in-love (Testimony 2), to rise in victory even in the face of extraordinary challenges. Their stories, along with many others not recorded in this book, are more than testimonies; they are living evidence of the absolute power of God. This kind of victory is not reserved for a select group of believers. It is the inheritance of every Christian who dares to trust God's ways.

Life, in its design, is not meant to be without battles - yet *for the believer*, every battle carries within it the *potential for victory*. The difference between defeat and triumph often lies in whether or not we have embraced Heaven's strategies for living victoriously.

Part One of this book is built on *foundational principles* that every believer **must** understand to walk in victory. These truths form the bedrock of the Christian's triumph. Part Two reveals the tactical applications of the spiritual truths found in Part One. It is a field manual for the believer - a collection of spiritual strategies drawn from Scripture that show us how to fight with Heaven's methods rather than human strength. Let me clearly state: no strategy in Part Two can succeed unless the principles in Part One have taken root in the heart. Principles give authority; strategies give movement. Principles establish identity; strategies express victory. Without the foundation, the structure cannot stand.

Before you begin this journey, I encourage you to pause and pray. Ask the Holy Spirit to speak to you beyond the words written on these pages. I am also human, so I write in part. Let Him reveal to you not only Heaven's principles but also Heaven's strategies. By the end of this book, I pray that you will not only know what victory looks like but live it - daily, boldly, and joyfully.

This is more than a book; it is a guide for warriors. May it awaken the fighter within you and remind you that through Christ you are not fighting for victory - you are fighting from it. You, dear child of God, are already victorious.

INTRO

I

INTRODUCTION

Before you journey into the pages of this book, it is important to understand three words that shape everything you are about to read: *principles, victory, and strategies.* These are not mere concepts; they are spiritual realities. They form the foundation, the promise, and the pathway of the believer's life. When you understand how these three work together, you begin to see why certain believers rise in strength and authority while others remain stuck in cycles of defeat. This book exists to break those cycles.

What Is a Principle?

A principle is a divine truth established by God, a spiritual law that does not change with time, emotion, or circumstance. A principle remains true whether you feel it, understand it, or apply it. It is the bedrock of the Kingdom of God. Principles explain what is true. They reveal how God designed victory to operate. You don't create principles; you discover them. You don't manipulate principles; you align with them.

In the context of this book, principles form the entire weight of

Part One. Identity, salvation, the Word, the Name of Jesus, the Blood, the Holy Spirit, a renewed mind, and a life of prayer, these are not suggestions. They are not ideas. They are not spiritual decorations. They are heavenly principles, eternal truths that carry victory within them.

Until you understand the principles of victory, you will always fight from weakness rather than authority. Everything God wants to build in your life rests upon these truths.

What Is Victory?

Victory is not a moment. It is not an event. It is not something you chase. Victory is a *position.* Victory is your birthright. Victory is a finished reality secured by Jesus Christ. When Jesus died and rose again, He did not give you potential victory, He gave you guaranteed victory. Victory is the atmosphere you were born into the day you were born again. It is the spiritual location from which every believer is meant to live, think, pray, and fight.

In this book, victory is defined as living daily from the finished work of Christ, fully aligned with who He is and who He has made you to be. You are not trying to win; you are enforcing what has already been won. You are not fighting for triumph; you are fighting from triumph. This is why understanding principles is so important: victory becomes unstable when it rests on emotion, but it becomes unshakable when it rests on truth.

As the book unfolds, you will discover that this victory extends across three vital arenas of your life: your spirit, your soul, and your physical world.

Part One establishes victory in the spirit - your identity, authority, and position in Christ. *Part Two* focuses on victory in the soul - bringing your mind, emotions, and desires into alignment with truth. *Part Three* reveals victory in the physical - practical, daily strategies that help you walk out what God has already secured.

What Is a Strategy?

If principles reveal what is true, strategies reveal how to walk in that truth. A strategy is a Spirit-led action, a divine method, a pattern of Heaven that teaches you how to move, position yourself, and respond in ways that unlock the power of the principles you have embraced. Strategies are not substitutes for principles; they are expressions of them.

Strategies take revelation and turn it into movement. Strategies take identity and turn it into impact. Strategies take truth and turn it into victory you can see, feel, and experience.

In the context of this book, strategies form Part Two. These strategies show you how to apply the eternal truths of Part One in daily battles, whether through obedience, consistency, silence, rest, focus, giving, service, or even divine reduction. They teach you why Heaven sometimes asks you to be still, sometimes to speak, sometimes to fight, and sometimes to step back. They show you how to cooperate with God's process so that His victory becomes your lifestyle.

How They Work Together

Now, hear this clearly: principles without strategies remain unused, and strategies without principles become powerless. Principles give you foundation; strategies give you motion. Principles establish your identity; strategies protect, sharpen, and apply that identity.

Principles define victory; strategies manifest victory. A house cannot stand without a foundation, but a foundation alone is not a house. Similarly, a believer cannot walk in victory with principles alone, you must learn Heaven's strategies. And you cannot walk in victory by strategies alone, you must stand on Heaven's principles.

This book is designed to give you both. Part One grounds you. Part Two guides you. Part One gives you the truths of Heaven. Part Two teaches you how to live those truths on earth. The strategies in Part Two cannot function without the principles in Part One. Identity must come before action. Foundation must come before movement. Revelation must come before application.

"But thanks be to God! He gives us the victory through our Lord Jesus Christ." - 1 Corinthians 15:57

Every believer is born into a battlefield. From the moment you gave your life to Christ, a spiritual war was declared against everything that reflects God in you. The Christian journey is not a passive walk but an active advance through territory that is often contested. Yet we advance with confidence - not because of our strength, but because Christ has already secured our victory.

My prayer is that as you read, your understanding will deepen, your spirit will awaken, and your posture will shift. May you step into the reality God always intended: a life built on eternal principles, empowered by divine strategies, and lived from unshakable victory.

As you begin this journey, open your heart fully to the Holy Spirit. Let Him anchor you in the principles, then empower you through the strategies. When principle and strategy unite, victory becomes your lived reality.

Welcome to *Heavenly Strategies for Victory*. May you walk boldly in the triumph Christ has already secured for you.

HEAVENLY STRATEGIES FOR VICTORY

BY

Bongani Maluka

Part One

VICTORY IN THE SPIRIT

CHAPTER

1

THE PRINCIPLE OF SALVATION

There is no real victory without salvation. When God planned humanity, He did not design us for defeat. From the very beginning, the will of God for His creation was dominion, not bondage, victory, not captivity. Yet the greatest tragedy of mankind was that sin entered the world and robbed us of the glory that was our inheritance. Humanity lost not just Eden, but identity, power, and relationship.

But because love never fails, God actioned a redemptive plan that would restore His children back to Himself - a plan sealed in blood and perfected in grace. Salvation is Heaven's first and greatest principle for victory. Every other victory we experience in life is built upon the foundation of salvation. *"For the Son of Man came to seek and to save that which was lost."* - Luke 19:10

Before one is saved, their greatest war is not against demons, poverty, or sickness - it is against sin. Sin is not just an act; it is a condition, a spiritual infection that separates man from his Source. In Eden, when Adam disobeyed, he did not merely eat fruit; he gave away his intimacy with God for independence, and in doing so, declared war against Heaven. From that moment, man lived defeated, because no one can win while disconnected from God.

Romans 3:23 tells us that *"all have sinned and fall short of the glory of God."* The glory referred to here is not just splendor or radiance; it is the victorious life of divine presence, the weight of God's presence in our lives. Sin stripped humanity of that glory. A life without God may appear successful outwardly but remains defeated inwardly. True victory begins not when circumstances change, but when the heart is reconciled to its Creator.

When Jesus stepped into the world, He did not come to decorate our defeats with religion. In other words, He did not come to merely offer religious practices and rituals that make our struggles more bearable and acceptable, He came to destroy the works of the enemy. He came to re-establish God's government within man's spirit. The cross, therefore, is not a symbol of weakness - it is Heaven's war banner of triumph. *"Having disarmed principalities and powers, He made a public spectacle of them, triumphing over them in it."* - Colossians 2:15

What Really Happened At The Cross?

At Calvary, a divine transaction took place. Our defeat was exchanged for His victory; our sin for His righteousness; our death for His life. The blood that flowed down from His side was not a tragic spill - it was an intentional release, purchasing back what had been stolen.

When Jesus cried out, *"It is finished,"* He was not announcing the end of His pain but the completion of our redemption. That moment marked **the transfer of power** from the hands of darkness back to the hands of the redeemed.

Salvation, therefore, is not a religious badge to identify believers; it is the legal restoration of man's authority on earth. Through salvation, we are reinstated as sons and daughters of the Most High, clothed again with glory, and equipped for victory. Many people see salvation as the end of a journey - as though it were the final stop before Heaven. But in truth, salvation is the beginning of all victory. It is the door that leads to every promise of God. Without salvation, no other spiritual weapon shared in this book can function effectively, because all authority flows from our union with Christ.

The cross is the greatest paradox of history. What looked like defeat - a dying man nailed to the cross - became the greatest victory ever recorded. At the cross, Satan celebrated too early, thinking that death had conquered life. But three days later, the grave became Heaven's pulpit, and the resurrection became the announcement of everlasting triumph.

Every believer must learn to see the cross not as a symbol of suffering but as a reminder of victory. When the enemy reminds you of your past, remind him of the cross. It was there that your record was erased. It was there that your victory was sealed.

"Therefore, if anyone is in Christ, he is a new creation; old things have passed away; behold, all things have become new." - 2 Corinthians 5:17. Salvation is not self-improvement; it is spiritual rebirth. God did not come to polish the old you; He came to create a new you. The old you was defeated by sin, but the new you is empowered by grace.

Your Victory Comes Through Relationship

Salvation is not merely an event; it is a restored relationship with our creator. Restored! Through Christ, we are reconciled to the Father, and reconciliation is the heartbeat of victory. Before, we were slaves to fear, bound by guilt and shame. Now, we are children of God, heirs of His promises, and citizens of His Kingdom.

Imagine a soldier who goes to war without communication with his commander - he is doomed to defeat. Likewise, a believer who claims salvation but avoids fellowship with God will always live beneath victory. The strength of salvation is intimacy. The closer you walk with God, the louder your victory resounds.

When you pray, when you worship, when you obey - you are not trying to earn favor; you are nurturing relationship. It is this relationship that becomes your fortress in times of battle. *"The name of the Lord is a strong tower; the righteous run to it and are safe."* - Proverbs 18:10. Victory through salvation means that your safety is no longer circumstantial - it is relational.

Your Victory is Guaranteed

My certainty of this victory isn't based on understanding every detail of the process, but purely on knowing Jesus, who makes that victory sure. Salvation guarantees victory, but many believers still live as though they are defeated. Why? Because the assurance of victory comes through faith, and faith is the key that unlocks what grace has provided. Grace provided salvation; faith activates it. Romans 10:9 declares, *"If you declare with your mouth, 'Jesus is Lord,' and believe in your heart that God raised him from the dead, you will be saved."* To believe is not just to agree intellectually; it is to submit practically. Salvation is not a ritual of recited words but a surrender of will. The believer who lives surrendered will always live victorious.

One of the devil's greatest tactics is to make believers doubt their salvation. If he can make you doubt that you are truly saved, he can make you live beneath your inheritance. But Jesus said in John 10:28, *"I give them eternal life, and they shall never perish; no one will snatch them out of My hand."* The security of salvation rests not in our ability to hold on to God, but in His power to hold on to us. When you understand that you are eternally held by the hands that conquered death, you begin to live boldly. You no longer approach life trembling but trusting. You no longer pray from fear but from faith.

Walking in the Newness of Life

After salvation comes transformation. Salvation is not the end of the story but the beginning of a journey. Every day becomes an opportunity to walk in the newness of life. Ephesians 4:22-24 instructs us to *"put off the old self, which is being corrupted by its deceitful desires; to be made new in the attitude of your minds; and to put on the new self, created to be like God in true righteousness and holiness."* To walk in victory, we must actively reject the old patterns that once ruled us. The habits, thoughts, and fears that defined our past cannot be allowed to define our redeemed life. As mentioned before, God did not save us to decorate our weaknesses; He saved us to display His strength through us.

This transformation is the ongoing work of sanctification - the process through which the Holy Spirit molds us into the image of Christ. Each victory we experience is evidence that the Spirit is still working, shaping, and perfecting us.

How do you know that you are truly saved? The evidence is victory. A saved life bears fruit; it reflects the nature of Christ. Salvation without change is pointless and without power. Jesus said in Matthew 7:20, *"By their fruits you shall know them."* The fruit of salvation is not perfection but progression. It is the visible growth from defeat to dominion, from bitterness to forgiveness, from fear to faith.

When salvation takes root, peace replaces anxiety, love conquers hatred, and hope silences despair. Your words change, your desires change, and even your company changes, because darkness and light cannot dwell together. If you find yourself struggling, do not be discouraged. The presence of struggle is not proof of defeat; it is evidence of transformation. Even a butterfly struggles within the cocoon before it flies.

You Can live The Victorious Life

The victorious life is a life that constantly draws from the finished work of Christ. To live victoriously, you must see yourself through Heaven's perspective. You are not a sinner trying to be righteous; you are the righteousness of God through Christ. You are not fighting for freedom; you are enforcing freedom that was already purchased.

Salvation redefines your position. You are seated with Christ in heavenly places (Ephesians 2:6). From this position, battles look smaller because you are looking from above, not below. Victory is maintained by continual dependence on God (I wrote at length about this in my book "becoming a child again"). When we begin to rely on ourselves, defeat creeps in. The devil does not fear your talent, your title, or your experience; he fears your salvation, because it ties you permanently to the One who already crushed him. Every time you declare, "I am saved," you are reminding hell of its defeat.

The Call to Salvation

Perhaps as you read this, you realize that you have admired Christ but never truly surrendered to Him. You know of Jesus, but you do not know Him. Salvation is available now. You do not need to clean yourself before coming to God; you come to Him so that He may cleanse you. If you have not yet received Jesus Christ as your Lord and Savior, pause and pray this prayer out loud:

Prayer of Salvation

Lord Jesus, I believe You are the Son of God. I believe You died for my sins and rose again for my justification. Today, I confess You as my Lord and Savior. Wash me with Your blood, fill me with Your Spirit, and write my name in the Book of Life. From this day forward, I belong to You. Amen.

If you prayed that prayer sincerely, Heaven rejoiced, and your victory has begun. *"Therefore being justified by faith, we have peace with God through our Lord Jesus Christ."* - Romans 5:1

Let's Recap

Salvation is Heaven's first principle for victory. It restores man to God. It replaces defeat with dominion. It establishes identity and authority. It guarantees eternal security and daily peace. Through salvation, you are not trying to escape hell - you are being restored to glory. The same Spirit that raised Jesus from the dead now dwells in you, empowering you to walk in victory every single day. No matter what life brings, remind yourself: I am saved, and salvation is my victory.

THE PRINCIPLE OF DIVINE IDENTITY

L et me first tell you a true story. There was a young man who thought he knew who he was, but he didn't. In high school, he built his identity around the people he admired. He idolized hip-hop artists. He dressed like them, spoke like them, and wanted to live like them. His language was foul, his goals were shallow, and his confidence was misplaced. He wanted to look successful, not to be whole, but to be seen.

He was good with words. He could battle anyone and win. He could write rhymes that turned heads and made people laugh or cheer. What he didn't know then was that his gift with words was not given to entertain, but to teach. The talent God placed in him was being misused, redirected toward an image that wasn't his to carry.

One day, a man came to his school and preached from Romans 6:1–4. He spoke about dying to sin and living for God. He spoke of a new life, a life hidden in Christ. The young man didn't understand a word of it. For someone who considered himself intelligent, that bothered him. He could easily dissect rap lyrics, memorize verses, and debate about life, but that message confused him. It stayed in his mind all day, stirring something he couldn't explain.

When the man finished preaching, he gave him a small, blue new testament Bible. He didn't know what to do with it at first. But something in him knew he had to find out what that scripture meant. The next Sunday, he found himself walking to church. He wasn't going there to worship, he was going to look for answers. He wanted to understand the scripture that had unsettled him. He didn't realize that, in that moment, God had already begun His work in him. Slowly, his desires started changing.

He received from the church more than what he was looking for. He began feeling uncomfortable with the lifestyle he once loved. The songs he used to enjoy began to irritate him. The words he once spoke so freely began to feel heavy. Even the way he dressed started to change, not because someone told him to, but because the person he was becoming no longer fit inside the image he had built.

It was subtle. Quiet. Almost unnoticeable at first. But one day he looked at himself and realized: he wasn't that same young man anymore. The chains were gone. The baggy jeans were gone. The arrogance was gone. In their place, there was peace. A new kind of confidence, not built on style or status, but on truth. The language of his life changed. He was no longer comfortable with what once defined him. The old identity had fallen away, and in its place, Christ was forming something new, something real. That's when he began to understand Romans 6. He didn't need to be like the people he admired. He needed to become the person God created.

That young man in the story, that was me. And it took an encounter with Christ to teach me that true victory begins when you stop trying to become someone else and start becoming who God says you are. The truth is, many believers find themselves caught in that same struggle. They know Jesus, but they don't really know who they are in Him. Just like I once did, they chase approval, imitate others, and measure themselves by the world's standards, unaware that they are already carrying Heaven's identity within them.

One of the greatest strategies of the enemy is confusion - not confusion of the mind, but confusion of identity. If he can make you forget who you are, he can make you forget what belongs to you. And when you do not know what belongs to you, you will live like a beggar in a palace built for kings. So in this chapter, I am going to do my best to help you be acquainted with who you truly are.

From the beginning of time, God's plan for man was not survival but dominion. You were never meant to live beneath, but above. Identity was the seal of that dominion. God said, *"Let us make man in our image, in our likeness, and let them have dominion..."* (Genesis 1:26). Identity came before assignment. Before God told Adam what to do, He told Adam who he was.

That is Heaven's order - you function effectively only when you know who you are. The tragedy of humanity is that sin not only separated man from God; it also separated man from his true self. The first thing lost in the fall of mankind in the garden of Eden was identity. The voice that once walked in the garden was now met with fear. When God asked, *"Where are you?"* (Genesis 3:9), He was not asking for Adam's location - He was asking about his position. "Where are you" meant "Where is the man I created in My image? Where is the authority, the confidence, the dominion?"

From that day, every human being born of Adam entered life with an identity crisis. But through Christ, God began a new lineage - a generation of those reborn into His likeness and restored to their rightful identity.

Identity Is the Foundation of Victory

You cannot win a battle you don't know you have authority in. A soldier who doubts his armor and weapons will never step boldly into war. Victory begins when you know who you are and whose you are. Satan's attack has always been against identity. Even in the wilderness, when Jesus fasted forty days, the devil's first temptation began with these words: *"If You are the Son of God..."* (Matthew 4:3). Notice - the devil didn't attack His power, His miracles, or His holiness. He attacked His identity.

Why? Because if he could make Jesus question who He was, he could make Him disobey who He was called to be. The same tactic is used today. The devil whispers: "If you were really saved, you wouldn't have fallen.", "If God truly loved you, this wouldn't have happened.", "If you were anointed, you wouldn't struggle like this." The aim is always to weaken your confidence in who you are in Christ, because when your identity shakes, your authority collapses.

But Jesus responded with the Word. He didn't debate; He declared. Identity must always be defended with Scripture. "It is written..." became His weapon - not because He didn't know who He was, but because He refused to let Satan define Him outside of what God had already said. You must do the same. The only safe place to discover and defend your identity is in the Word of God. Everything else is a lie. Again, Everything else is a lie!

You Are Who God Says You Are

Identity is not built on emotions; it is built on revelation. Feelings change, situations shift, but the Word of God is eternal. In John 1:12, the Bible declares, *"But as many as received Him, to them He gave power to become the sons of God, even to them that believe on His name."* Please hear me out: You did not make yourself a child of God - God made you one. Salvation gave you more than forgiveness; it gave you a new identity. You are not what you used to be. You are not the sum of your mistakes. You are not defined by your past or your pain. You are a child of the King.

Paul says in 2 Corinthians 5:17, *"If anyone is in Christ, he is a new creation; old things have passed away; behold, all things have become new."* This is not poetry; it is divine reality. You were not rehabilitated; you were re-created. The old you that was defeated no longer exists - you were born again into victory. When you accepted Christ, Heaven issued you a new identity card. You received a new name, a new citizenship, and a new inheritance. Your spiritual DNA changed. You now carry the bloodline of Jesus Christ. That means defeat is no longer in your spiritual genetics. You were designed for victory.

Adopted into Sonship

One of the most beautiful truths of Scripture is adoption. Romans 8:15 says, *"For you did not receive the spirit of bondage again to fear, but you received the Spirit of adoption by whom we cry out, 'Abba, Father!'"* In Roman culture, adoption was not a casual term; it was legal and irreversible. An adopted child could never be disowned. He had full access to inheritance as if he were born biologically. That is what God did for us. Through Christ, we were adopted into His family - legally restored and spiritually secured.

This means your victory is not something you earn; it's your family heritage. Every child of God is born into victory because our Father has never lost a battle. When the prodigal son returned home (Luke 15), he tried to come back as a servant. He said, *"I am no longer worthy to be called your son."* But the father interrupted him and said, *"Bring the best robe, put a ring on his hand, and sandals on his feet."* The father was saying, "Your mistakes do not cancel your identity."

That's the heart of God - identity restored before explanation. The son was still dirty, but the father saw destiny. Likewise, even when you fail, God doesn't see you through the lens of your sin; He sees you through the blood of His Son.

Authority Flows from Identity

When you understand your identity, authority becomes natural. Authority is not loudness; it is rootedness in identity. A police officer can stop traffic not because he is stronger than the car, but because of the authority behind his uniform. Likewise, a believer walks in spiritual authority not because of personal strength but because of divine backing.

Luke 10:19 says, *"Behold, I give you authority to trample on serpents and scorpions, and over all the power of the enemy, and nothing shall by any means hurt you."* Notice the distinction - the enemy has power, but you have authority. Power moves things, but authority commands power. The devil may have power, but he has no legal right over a believer who knows their identity.

Authority is only effective when identity is established. The seven sons of Sceva in Acts 19 tried to cast out demons by saying, *"In the name of Jesus whom Paul preaches."* The demon replied, *"Jesus I know, and Paul I know; but who are you?"* (Acts 19:15). The question of the spirit world is not what you know, but who you are. When you do not know who you are, you are powerless even when you know what is right.

Victory through identity means walking with the consciousness that you represent Heaven on earth. You are God's ambassador, and ambassadors do not speak their own opinions - they declare the will of the one who sent them. So in the next few minutes, I will share with you, some truths about Identity.

1. Identity Brings Stability

A believer who is unsure of their identity will always live an unstable life. One day they feel victorious; the next, defeated. One day they believe they are loved; the next, they question God's goodness.

James 1:6 warns that *"the one who doubts is like a wave of the sea, blown and tossed by the wind."* When your identity is grounded in Christ, you remain steady even when storms rise. You no longer interpret God's love through your circumstances but through the cross.

When you know who you are, storms no longer define you; they refine you. You begin to see challenges as opportunities for God to reveal His strength in you.

Remember Daniel in Babylon. Though he was taken captive, he never lost his sense of identity. He purposed in his heart not to defile himself (Daniel 1:8). He knew he was a child of the covenant, not a slave of circumstance. His identity preserved his integrity, and his integrity produced his victory. Some of your victories in your business dealings will come because you know that you are a child of the covenant – You do not take bribes or shortcuts.

Likewise, Joseph's identity as a man of God preserved him through betrayal, false accusation, and imprisonment. Even in prison, he interpreted dreams. Identity doesn't fade in adversity; it shines brighter.

2. Identity Produces Confidence

When you are sure of who you are, fear loses its grip. Hebrews 10:35 says, *"Do not throw away your confidence; it will be richly rewarded."* Confidence is the posture of faith. David understood this. When everyone else saw a giant, David saw an opportunity. He didn't see himself as a shepherd boy; he saw himself as a covenant child. His words were clear: *"Who is this uncircumcised Philistine that he should defy the armies of the living God?"* (1 Samuel 17:26). David's confidence didn't come from his sling; it came from his identity. He knew he was in covenant with God, and covenant means guaranteed backing.

The same is true for you. When you step into prayer, do not see yourself as a helpless sinner begging for mercy; see yourself as a child approaching a loving Father. You are not tolerated in Heaven's courts - you are celebrated.

3. Identity Restores Purpose

The moment you discover who you are, you also discover why you are here. Purpose flows from identity. A pen's purpose is found in its design - it writes. Likewise, your purpose is found in your divine design.

Ephesians 2:10 says, *"For we are His workmanship, created in Christ Jesus for good works, which God prepared beforehand that we should walk in them."* You are not an accident; you are a divine project. The same God who saved you also assigned you. When you live without identity, you live without direction. The world will try to label you, define you, and limit you. But the Word reminds us that we are chosen, royal, holy, and peculiar (1 Peter 2:9). Peculiar means "set apart," not "strange." You were not designed to fit in; you were designed to stand out.

Identity empowers you to walk in purpose boldly. You begin to realize that your existence is divine strategy - you were placed where you are for victory's sake.

The Dangers of a Lost Identity

A believer who forgets their identity becomes vulnerable. The devil cannot steal your salvation, but he can steal your confidence in it. That's why identity theft in the spirit is one of his oldest tricks.

Eve fell not because she was weak, but because she was deceived about her identity. The serpent said, *"You will be like God,"* ignoring that she was already created in God's image. The lie of Satan is always to make you chase what you already have.

When you forget your identity, you start competing with others instead of completing your purpose. You start performing for acceptance instead of resting in grace. You start living in fear instead of walking in authority. Identity confusion produces defeat, but identity revelation produces dominion.

So, who are you?

I am glad you asked that question, "who am I in Christ?" should be the first question every believer asks themselves, daily. See, when you view yourself through your past, you limit yourself only to that past. When you see yourself through Christ, you live in revelation of what you already are. Every believer must learn to see themselves as God sees them, not through the eyes of guilt, failure, or comparison, but through the eyes of grace and truth.

The book of Ephesians paints one of the clearest pictures of who we are in Christ. It is more than a letter; it is a mirror. Paul doesn't write about what we must become; he writes about what we already are.

Let's take a moment to look into that mirror.

1.   You Are Chosen

"For He chose us in Him before the foundation of the world, to be holy and blameless in His sight." - Ephesians 1:4

Before the world had a name, God had already called yours. You were not an afterthought; you were chosen on purpose, for purpose. This means you are not defined by rejection, disappointment, or failure - you are chosen. Every time you doubt your worth, remember: you are wanted by God. The One who knows everything about you, even your worst, still calls you His own.

This truth silences the voice of insecurity that says, *"You're not enough."* When that thought comes, remind yourself - I am chosen.

If you don't get the job you wanted or the approval you sought, don't crumble - you were chosen before any opportunity existed.

When others overlook you, Heaven does not. God's choosing gives your life meaning even when people don't see your value.

2. You Are Adopted

"In love He predestined us for adoption to sonship through Jesus Christ." - Ephesians 1:5

Adoption means belonging. It means you have a Father who takes responsibility for you. Through Christ, you are no longer an orphan wandering through life; you are part of a royal family. Adoption is not about behavior - it's about birthright. You don't earn it; you inherit it. God didn't just save you to keep you at a distance; He brought you into His household. So when the enemy whispers that you are alone, remind him: I have a Father, and His Spirit calls me son (or daughter).

This means you never have to live with the orphan mindset - that fear of being unwanted, unnoticed, or unprotected. When life gets hard and you're tempted to say, "No one cares about me," stop and remember: you are adopted. God has taken ownership of you and your future. You are not fending for yourself anymore. He's the Father who provides, protects, and prepares. When you pray, you're not begging a distant deity - you're talking to your heavenly Father, who truly cares about you, and every little detail about your life.

3. You Are Redeemed and Forgiven

"In Him we have redemption through His blood, the forgiveness of sins." - Ephesians 1:7

Redemption means "to buy back." You were purchased at the highest price - the blood of Jesus. This means your past no longer has authority over your present. You are not bound by what you did; you are freed by what He did. Forgiveness doesn't excuse sin; it erases it. When God forgives, He doesn't keep a record - He removes it. To live redeemed is to walk as someone who knows that guilt no longer has a voice in Heaven's court.

When the enemy brings up your past, don't argue - agree with truth. "Yes, that was me, but that person no longer exists." You don't have to keep punishing yourself for what Jesus already paid for. Let go of shame. Stop replaying the old failures in your mind. The Blood has already spoken your acquittal. If you stumble, don't run from God - run to Him. The price for your redemption has already been paid in full.

4. You Are Sealed by the Holy Spirit

"When you believed, you were marked in Him with a seal, the promised Holy Spirit." - Ephesians 1:13

Every believer carries Heaven's mark. The Holy Spirit is the seal of ownership and assurance. His presence in your life is proof that you belong to God and that your salvation is secure. You don't need to prove yourself to the world or anyone. Heaven has already stamped you with its seal. That seal means: You are His. You are protected. You are preserved.

When doubt comes, remember the seal. The Holy Spirit's presence is your reminder that you are not doing this walk alone. It's like having a spiritual passport - proof of citizenship wherever you go. When you feel far from God, pause and listen - His Spirit is still within you, guiding and comforting you. Even when you fall short, the seal doesn't break. You don't lose your salvation because of weakness; you are kept by His faithfulness.

5. You Are Made Alive and Raised with Christ

"But because of His great love for us, God, who is rich in mercy, made us alive with Christ... and raised us up with Him and seated us with Him in the heavenly realms." - Ephesians 2:4-6

Your identity is not just forgiven; it's resurrected. You were not simply made better - you were made new. God didn't clean up your old life; He gave you a new one. You were raised with Christ to live above sin, fear, and condemnation. When you realize where you are seated - with Him - your perspective changes. You stop fighting from the ground and start reigning from His throne.

This means that sin no longer defines you. You may fall, but you don't live there. When anxiety or fear tries to chain you down, remember where you sit - above, not beneath. In moments of pressure, remind yourself: "I am seated with Christ."

That's not arrogance - that's spiritual reality. You're not looking up at your problems; you're looking down on them from a place of authority. When you pray, pray from that seat. You're not a beggar at the gate - you're a child at the table.

6. You Are God's Masterpiece

"For we are His workmanship, created in Christ Jesus for good works, which God prepared beforehand for us to do." - Ephesians 2:10

You are not an accident. You are God's design, intentionally shaped for purpose. The Greek word for workmanship is poiēma, from which we get the word poem. That means you are God's poem - His creative expression on the earth. Every believer is uniquely crafted to reveal a piece of God's glory. You don't need to imitate anyone; you were made to represent Him in your own way. When you understand that you are God's masterpiece, you stop striving for perfection and start walking in purpose.

This means your uniqueness is your strength, not your flaw. Stop comparing your journey to others - you carry a verse of God's poetry they don't have. Maybe your calling is to preach, to parent, to design, to build - whatever it is, it's divine. When you start to feel ordinary, remind yourself: there is nothing ordinary about being God's masterpiece.

7. You Are a Citizen of Heaven

You are no longer foreigners and strangers, but fellow citizens with God's people and members of His household." - Ephesians 2:19

Your citizenship has changed. You may live on earth, but your home is Heaven. That means your standards, your culture, and your values come from above. You don't fit in with the world because you weren't made for it - you were made to transform it. You are an ambassador of the Kingdom, representing Heaven in every sphere of life. When people see you, they should catch a glimpse of the One who sent you.

This means you live by Heaven's principles even when the world disagrees. When others cheat to get ahead, you choose integrity because you serve a higher government. When others live for temporary applause, you live for eternal reward. As a citizen of Heaven, your job is to make the culture of Heaven visible on earth - through kindness, honesty, and love. You represent the King wherever you go.

Identity and the Mind

Victory through identity also requires renewal of the mind. Romans 12:2 teaches, "*Do not be conformed to this world, but be transformed by the renewing of your mind.*" When you got saved, your spirit was instantly changed, but your mind must be renewed daily. If the mind still believes lies, the heart cannot walk in truth. The battle for identity is fought in the mind. We will cover this in detail in a later section of this book. Every thought that says, "you can't," "you're not worthy," or "you'll never make it" is a lie from the pit of hell.

You overcome lies by replacing them with truth. Speak the Word aloud until your mind begins to believe what your spirit already knows. Say to yourself: I am a child of God (John 1:12). I am chosen, holy, and beloved (Colossians 3:12). I am the righteousness of God in Christ (2 Corinthians 5:21). I am seated with Christ in heavenly places (Ephesians 2:6). Identity must be spoken before it is seen.

The Fruit of Identity

When you walk in identity, victory becomes effortless. You stop trying to prove yourself and start resting in what Christ has already proven. Your prayers change. You no longer beg for what is yours; you declare it with authority.

A believer who knows their identity prays differently, praises differently, and lives differently. They do not panic when storms come because they know the one who calms the storm lives within them. Galatians 2:20 summarizes it beautifully: "*I have been crucified with Christ; it is no longer I who live, but Christ lives in me.*" The victorious life is the exchanged life - His strength for your weakness, His wisdom for your confusion, His peace for your anxiety.

The fruit of identity is seen in how one begins to serve and obey God as a son, not a slave. There is a vast difference between serving God as a slave and serving Him as a son. Slaves obey out of fear; sons obey out of love. Slaves work for acceptance; sons work from acceptance.

When you live as a son, obedience is not burdensome because love fuels it. You know that your Father's correction is not rejection. You live free, joyful, and victorious. The story of Mephibosheth in 2 Samuel 9 captures this perfectly. He was crippled, forgotten, and living in exile. Yet King David remembered his covenant with Jonathan and called him to the palace. Mephibosheth bowed and said, *"What is your servant, that you should look upon such a dead dog as I?"* But David restored all that belonged to him and gave him a permanent seat at the king's table. You would need to realize that Mephibosheth was not as ordinary as he saw himself, he was of royal blood. This is the case with most of us. We see ourselves as ordinary, whereas God has made us Kings (*Revelations 5:10*). Just like David, God has invited us into a permanent seat at the table of Kings, that's who you are!

That is grace. That is identity. Though crippled by sin, you have been invited to dine with the King. You are no longer an outcast; you are family.

Let's Recap

Victory through identity means living with divine awareness of who you are in Christ. Identity was lost through sin but restored through salvation. Satan's main weapon is confusion; God's main strategy is revelation. Authority flows naturally from identity.

Confidence, stability, and purpose are fruits of a secure identity. You are not trying to become victorious - you already are, because your identity is anchored in the Victor Himself. When you truly know who you are, no battle can intimidate you, no failure can define you, and no enemy can defeat you. For you have been made more than a conqueror through Him who loves you (Romans 8:37).

So, stand tall, child of God. Lift your head and your hands up to heaven because heaven recognizes your name. You are blood-bought, Spirit-filled, and victory-marked. You were never created for defeat.

Your identity is your victory. This is who you are, know it, embrace it, live it, walk in it.

A Prayer for Victory Through Identity

Father, thank You for calling me Your child and for giving me a new identity in Christ. I renounce every lie that has ever told me I am less than who You created me to be. Today I receive the truth that I am chosen, redeemed, forgiven, and loved. Help me to see myself through Your eyes and to walk in the confidence of who I am in You.

Holy Spirit, remind me daily that my worth is not in what I do but in Whose I am. Strengthen me to live as a reflection of Your Kingdom - secure, bold, and unashamed. Teach me to stand firm in the identity You have given me, so that my life reveals Jesus in every word, every action, and every victory. In His mighty name I pray, Amen.

CHAPTER

3

THE PRINCIPLE OF OBEDIENCE

"If you are willing and obedient, you shall eat the good of the land."
- Isaiah 1:19

Obedience is the forgotten key that unlocks the door to divine victory. In a world that glorifies independence and personal will, obedience sounds like a limitation. Yet in the Kingdom of God, obedience is not bondage - it is freedom. It is the bridge between promise and possession, between revelation and manifestation.

God's power is always available, but it only flows where obedience has created a channel. You may pray, fast, and declare the Word, but without obedience, none of these can bear lasting fruit. For in the Kingdom, victory is not achieved through effort but through alignment. When we talk about victory, many imagine the power to command demons or to perform miracles - and that is part of it - but the highest form of victory is the victory over one's own will. To obey God when it is hard, when it hurts, or when it makes no sense, is to declare that His Lordship is greater than our logic.

Obedience is Heaven's strategy for divine authority. The most anointed men and women in Scripture were not those with the greatest talent, or those with the greatest displays of power, but those with the greatest obedience. Every mighty move of God was preceded by a simple act of obedience. From Abraham leaving his homeland to Noah building an ark in the desert; from Moses stretching his staff over the Red Sea to Peter casting his net after a night of failure - obedience has always been the difference between ordinary and supernatural outcomes.

Victory through obedience is not just a principle; it is a lifestyle. So let me share with you some truths about obedience that I believe will help you understand obedience in order to be a victorious believer.

1.   Obedience Is Proof of Love

"If you love Me, keep My commandments." - John 14:15

True obedience is born not out of fear, but out of love. The true test of your love for God is in how much you obey His commands. Religion obeys to avoid punishment, but relationship obeys to bring pleasure to the One loved. The heart that truly loves God does not struggle to submit to Him.

When you love God deeply, obedience becomes a joy, not a burden. You stop seeing God's commands as restrictions and start seeing them as protection. Every instruction from God is an expression of His love and a pathway to your victory. Adam and Eve's fall was not because of ignorance; it was because of disobedience. They heard God clearly but chose another voice.

Likewise, many believers are not defeated by lack of prayer or knowledge, but by selective obedience. We obey when it benefits us and delay when it costs us. Love-driven obedience does not negotiate; it trusts. Abraham did not argue with God about Isaac. The Bible says he rose early in the morning (Genesis 22:3). Love moves quickly when God speaks.

If obedience is the proof of love, disobedience is the proof of mistrust. Every time we disobey, we are silently saying, "Dear God, I think my way is safer and better than Yours." And yet, the most dangerous place in the world is outside the will of God. When we walk in obedience, we position ourselves under divine protection. Love obeys because love trusts that the Father knows best.

2. Obedience Is the Language of Faith

Faith and obedience are two sides of the same coin. You cannot claim to have faith in God while refusing to obey His Word. True faith always expresses itself in obedience.

Hebrews 11 - the great "Hall of Faith" - is actually a record of obedient men and women. By faith, Noah built; by faith, Abraham went; by faith, Moses forsook Egypt; by faith, Rahab hid the spies. Faith was not passive belief; it was active obedience. James says, *"Faith without works is dead."* (James 2:17). To say "I believe" but do nothing about what you believe is to live in deception. Faith gives birth to obedience, and obedience gives birth to victory.

Peter's miracle was not in the net, but in the obedience to cast it one more time. He said, *"Master, we have toiled all night and caught nothing, but at Your word I will let down the net."* The phrase "at Your word" is the anthem of every victorious believer. Obedience is doing what God says, even when it defies logic. Faith begins where reasoning ends.

49

3. Obedience Is Better Than Understanding

We often delay obedience because we want full explanations. We want to understand every detail before we act. But God does not owe us explanations; He gives us instructions.

When God told Abraham to leave his country, He didn't give him a map - only a promise. *"Go to the land I will show you."* (Genesis 12:1). Abraham obeyed, not because he understood, but because he trusted. That obedience birthed a nation. Many times, God's instructions won't make sense. Naaman was told to dip seven times in the Jordan River to be healed of leprosy (2 Kings 5). At first, he was offended - *"Are not the rivers of Damascus better?"* he asked. But when he finally obeyed, his healing came instantly.

4. Obedience Is a Test of Humility

Pride resists obedience because obedience requires one to surrender. The humble heart says, *"Not my will, but Yours be done."* (Luke 22:42). Even Jesus - though He was the Son of God - *"learned obedience by the things which He suffered."* (Hebrews 5:8). If the perfect Son had to learn obedience, how much more must we?

Humility and obedience walk hand in hand. Pride says, "I know better." Humility says, "God knows best." God lifts the obedient because obedience honors His sovereignty. Philippians 2:8-9 tells us that Jesus *"became obedient to the point of death - even death on a cross. Therefore, God exalted Him and gave Him the name above every name."* (We will revisit this in a later victory chapter) Exaltation followed obedience.

You may not always understand God's methods, but His motives are always pure. Obedience does not require comprehension; it

50

requires submission. In the Kingdom, understanding follows obedience, not the other way around. The light comes after you step forward in faith.

If you want to rise in victory, bow first. The path to victory always passes through submission.

What is the reward for Obedience?

Every act of obedience carries a divine reward. God never asks you to obey without preparing a blessing in return

Deuteronomy 28 opens with a powerful promise: *"And it shall come to pass, if you shall hearken diligently unto the voice of the Lord your God, to observe and to do all His commandments which I command you this day, that the Lord your God will set you high above all nations of the earth."* Obedience lifts. It promotes. It prospers. When you obey, Heaven endorses your steps. You become untouchable by circumstances because your life is governed by divine instruction.

Abraham's obedience made him a friend of God. The widow of Zarephath's obedience to feed Elijah in famine sustained her household. Mary's obedience to God's Word made her the vessel of the Savior. Every testimony in Scripture has obedience at its root. You cannot separate divine manifestation from human cooperation. When your obedience is complete, your victory is guaranteed.

Obedience Unlocks Divine Direction

One of the greatest gifts of obedience is that it unlocks divine guidance. Psalm 32:8 declares, *"I will instruct you and teach you in the way you should go; I will counsel you with My loving eye on you."*

God reveals the next step only to those who have obeyed the last one. Many cry out for new instructions, but Heaven is still waiting for obedience to the previous command. When Abraham obeyed and offered Isaac, God revealed a ram in the thicket. Provision follows obedience. When Israel followed the pillar of cloud and fire, they never missed their route. Direction is not a mystery to the obedient heart. If you feel lost, return to the last thing God told you to do. Obedience restores clarity.

Obedience Brings Peace

When you live in obedience, peace becomes your portion. There is no anxiety in a surrendered heart. Anxiety comes from wanting to have control over what you shouldn't be controlling. Isaiah 26:3 promises, *"You will keep him in perfect peace, whose mind is stayed on You, because he trusts in You."*

Disobedience creates inner turmoil because the conscience cannot find rest outside of God's will. But when you obey, peace follows - even when the outcome is uncertain. Noah had peace building an ark in the desert. Daniel had peace praying in defiance of the king's law. Jesus had peace going to the cross, because obedience anchors the soul in the will of God.

Obedience in Small Things

We often think obedience is only about big sacrifices, but God tests us in the small instructions. It's the daily decisions - forgiving when it hurts, giving when it's hard, serving when it's unseen - that prepare us for greater victories.

Luke 16:10 says, *"He who is faithful in what is least is faithful also in much."* David obeyed in the field before he was trusted with the throne. Joshua served under Moses faithfully before he led Israel. Obedience in secret qualifies you for promotion in public. Every small "yes" you give to God builds a foundation for major breakthroughs. Don't wait for a dramatic command to start obeying; victory begins with daily submission.

So, what is the cost of Disobedience?

Disobedience carries a high price - it is expensive beyond measure. The Bible is filled with examples of people who lost everything simply because they ignored divine instructions. King Saul is a striking example. God had instructed him to destroy Amalek completely, but Saul chose partial obedience. He spared the best sheep and cattle, claiming he wanted to sacrifice them to God. But partial obedience is full disobedience in Heaven's eyes.

Samuel's words echo through time: *"To obey is better than sacrifice, and to heed is better than the fat of rams."* (1 Samuel 15:22). Saul lost his crown that day, not because he lacked courage, but because he lacked obedience.

Many Christians today are spiritually frustrated, wondering why they are not seeing God's promises fulfilled. They pray for breakthroughs, but Heaven is waiting for one simple act of obedience. It is not that God is silent; He is waiting for alignment. Disobedience disconnects us from divine flow. It shuts the gate of favor and opens the door of delay. Jonah learned this the hard way. When God sent him to Nineveh, he ran in the opposite direction. The result was chaos - a storm, fear, and time wasted in the belly of a fish. But when he finally obeyed, the same God who disciplined him delivered him.

Disobedience does not only cost us; it affects others connected to us. The sailors with Jonah suffered the storm because of his rebellion. When a believer disobeys, their household, ministry, or even community can experience the ripple effects. Obedience may cost you something, but disobedience will cost you everything.

The Ultimate Example of Obedience

At the center of our faith stands the cross - the ultimate picture of obedience. Jesus could have chosen comfort over the cross, but He submitted. His obedience brought salvation to all mankind.

Romans 5:19 says, *"For as by one man's disobedience many were made sinners, so also by one Man's obedience many will be made righteous."* Through Christ, obedience conquered rebellion. The same Spirit that empowered Jesus to obey lives in us today, enabling us to walk in continual victory.

Every time you choose obedience, you echo the obedience of Christ. You declare to the world that His Spirit reigns in you.

Let's Recap

Victory through obedience is not a one-time event; it is a lifestyle of submission to the will of God. Obedience is the proof of love and the language of faith. Disobedience disconnects us from divine flow and delays destiny.

True obedience does not wait for full understanding; it trusts God's character. Every act of obedience carries a reward - in peace, provision, and promotion. The greatest example of obedience is Jesus, whose submission brought salvation.

When you walk in obedience, you walk in alignment with Heaven. And wherever there is alignment, there is authority. Your victory is hidden in your obedience. Every time you say "Yes, Lord," Heaven moves on your behalf. Victory is eminent!

A Prayer for Obedience

Father, thank You for teaching me the power of obedience. Give me a heart that yields quickly to Your voice. Break every stubbornness within me and replace it with submission. Help me to trust even when I do not understand. May my obedience speak louder than my words, and may my life bring glory to You. In Jesus' name, amen.

CHAPTER

4

THE PRINCIPLE OF THE DIVINE WORD

"For the word of God is living and active. Sharper than any double-edged sword, it penetrates even to dividing soul and spirit, joints and marrow; it judges the thoughts and attitudes of the heart." - Hebrews 4:12

All victorious believers have one thing in common: a deep relationship with the Word of God. The Word is not merely a book; it is a weapon. It is not a collection of ancient writings; it is the very breath of God printed on paper. Everything God has ever done, and everything He will ever do, begins and ends with His Word.

In the Kingdom of God, victory is not achieved by might, status, or eloquence - it is achieved through the Word. God's Word is both the seed of life and the sword of warfare. Without it, prayer becomes powerless, faith becomes weak, and obedience becomes impossible. The Word of God is the foundation upon which all victory stands.

When we speak of "the Word," we speak of two divine expressions: the Logos and the Rhema. Both are vital, both are powerful, and both are essential for victorious living. The Logos is the written Word - the revealed truth of Scripture. The Rhema is the spoken or revealed Word - a specific Word from God spoken by the Holy Spirit to your spirit for a specific time or situation.

In this chapter, we will learn how both work together to produce victory, how to engage them in battle, and how to live by them daily. For man shall not live by bread alone, but by every Word that proceeds from the mouth of God (Matthew 4:4).

Understanding God's Eternal Voice – The Word!

Before time began, before creation existed, there was the Word. John 1:1 declares, *"In the beginning was the Word, and the Word was with God, and the Word was God."*

This is one of the most profound truths in all of Scripture - the Word is not separate from God; the Word is God. This means when you hold your Bible, you hold the mind, the will, and the authority of God in written form. The Bible is not man's opinion about God; it is God's revelation of Himself to man.

The Word is eternal, unchanging, and powerful. Heaven and earth will pass away, but the Word of God will never pass away (Matthew 24:35). Kings rise and fall, cultures evolve, but God's Word stands unshaken. When God speaks, things happen. The entire universe came into being through His Word: *"And God said, 'Let there be light,' and there was light."* (Genesis 1:3). The creative force behind everything visible is an invisible Word.

The same Word that created the world still creates possibilities in the life of the believer. When you speak the Word in faith, you are not reciting - you are creating. Every time the Word leaves your lips,

Heaven moves to confirm it. This is why it is so important for understand what this word is.

Guess what, this same word, reveals all we need to know about it. It comes to our lives in two harmonic ways:

The Logos: The Written Word

The Logos is the written, established Word of God - the Scriptures. It is the general revelation of God's truth that applies to all believers across all generations. The Logos reveals who God is, what He has done, and what He expects of His children.

When we read the Bible, we are not just reading history; we are feeding our spirit. The Logos is the spiritual food that nourishes the believer. Without it, faith starves. Romans 10:17 teaches, *"Faith comes by hearing, and hearing by the Word (Logos) of God."* Many Christians struggle to live victoriously because their spirit is malnourished. They read the Bible occasionally or only when in trouble. But victory requires a lifestyle of meditation, not a moment of panic.

Joshua 1:8 gives the key to victory: *"Keep this Book of the Law always on your lips; meditate on it day and night, so that you may be careful to do everything written in it. Then you will make your way prosperous and have good success."* Meditation turns information into revelation. Reading gives you knowledge; meditation gives you understanding. The Logos becomes powerful when it is internalized.

When the Word fills your heart, it shapes your thoughts, aligns your desires, and directs your steps. You begin to think like God, speak like God, and respond like God. That is how victory becomes natural - you are living from the inside out, not reacting from the outside in. The Logos is your foundation. It grounds you when storms come. It reminds you of who God is when feelings fade.

The Rhema: The Revealed Word

While the Logos is the written Word, the Rhema is the spoken or quickened Word - a personal word from God revealed to your spirit through the Holy Spirit.

The Rhema Word is when Scripture leaps off the page and speaks directly to your situation. It is when a verse you've read a hundred times suddenly becomes alive and specific. It's when the Holy Spirit whispers, "This is for you, now."

Ephesians 6:17 says, *"Take the sword of the Spirit, which is the Word (Rhema) of God."* Notice - in spiritual warfare, it is not the general Logos that cuts the enemy; it is the Rhema - the spoken, active Word. When Jesus was tempted in the wilderness, He didn't argue with the devil; He declared, *"It is written!"* (Matthew 4:4, 7, 10). That was Rhema - the Spirit-breathed Word released with authority for that specific situation.

Rhema is the Word in motion. It is when the Holy Spirit takes a portion of the Logos and breathes life into it for your now-moment. When you face sickness, and the Spirit quickens Isaiah 53:5 - *"By His stripes you are healed"* - that becomes Rhema, and it carries healing power because it is no longer just text; it is a divine decree. The more you fill yourself with Logos, the more material the Holy Spirit has to produce Rhema from. Without Logos, there can be no Rhema, because the Spirit reminds you of what God has already said (John 14:26). Rhema is what transforms Scripture into strategy.

What is "The Word"?

A victorious life begins with understanding the power of the weapon every believer holds in their hand - the Word!

How many times have you sat in church, heard a powerful message that stirred your heart, and thought, "This is so good, I'll never forget it," only to realize two days later that you can't remember a thing that was said? How many times have you walked out of the service fired up to apply the Word, only to find that the fire faded before the week even ended?

That's not coincidence - it's strategy. The enemy knows that if he can steal the Word from your heart, he has disarmed you. He knows that once the Word is forgotten, the believer is left standing in a battlefield without a weapon - fully present, but powerless.

So let's take a closer look at this powerful weapon called the Word and discover why it is essential to your victory.

1. The Word as a Weapon For War

The Word of God is not only for study and comfort - it is for battle. Scripture calls it a sword, not a pillow. (I am reminded of one of my mentors, Apostle Manyaka, who at the writing of this book, I received news about his passing. May his rest in peace.) He used to say, "The devil is here to kill you, not to kiss you", therefore you need to carry your sword. In Ephesians 6:17, Paul lists it as part of the believer's armor: *"Take the helmet of salvation and the sword of the Spirit, which is the Word of God."*

A sword must be used to be effective. Many believers carry the Bible but never wield it. It is not the Bible on your shelf that brings victory; it is the Word in your mouth and heart. When Satan attacks, do not respond with emotions - respond with Scripture. When fear rises, declare, "God has not given me a spirit of fear." When lack threatens, speak, *The Lord is my Shepherd; I shall not want.* When sickness whispers defeat, declare, "*By His stripes I am healed.*"

The Word is your offensive weapon. It cuts through lies, breaks strongholds, and dismantles the arguments of the enemy. It is written in Jeremiah 23:29, *"Is not My word like fire,"* declares the Lord, *"and like a hammer that breaks the rock in pieces?* When you speak the Word, you release fire and break every rock of resistance.

2. The Word as A Mind Renewal Agent

Victory begins in the mind. Before you can win outwardly, you must win inwardly. The Word is God's tool for renewing your thinking.

Romans 12:2 commands, *"Do not be conformed to this world, but be transformed by the renewing of your mind."* The Word reprograms your thoughts from fear to faith, from doubt to confidence, from defeat to dominion. The world trains us to think according to facts; the Word trains us to think according to truth. Facts change; truth does not.

When David faced Goliath, others saw an unbeatable giant, but David's mind was renewed by the Word of covenant. He said, *"Who is this uncircumcised Philistine?"* In other words, "Who is this man without covenant rights defying God's people?" That mindset is what produces victory. When your mind is filled with God's Word, problems lose their intimidation. You begin to see them from Heaven's perspective.

Every battle is first a battle of belief. The devil's greatest war is against your mind because whoever controls your thoughts controls your life. But when your mind is filled with Scripture, you become unshakable.

3. The Word as a Faith Building Agent

I didn't write a lot about faith in this book, not because it is not important to your victory but because, in principle, your focus in God's word will always birth faith. Faith is the oxygen of victory, and the Word is the breath that gives faith life.

Romans 10:17 says, *"Faith comes by hearing, and hearing by the Word of God."* That means the more you hear, speak, and meditate on the Word, the stronger your faith becomes. Faith doesn't grow by wishing; it grows by feeding. When you consistently hear the Word, it begins to dominate your thinking. The voice of fear grows faint, and the voice of truth grows louder.

Even in the darkest valley, faith reminds you of God's promises. The Word becomes an anchor in the storm. It says, "He who promised is faithful." The Word of God is like fuel - it keeps your faith engine running. Without it, prayer feels empty, and hope fades. With it, even mountains move.

4. The Word as a Constant, even in Trials

When life gets difficult, emotions fluctuate, but the Word remains firm. Jesus said in Matthew 7:24, *"Whoever hears these words of mine and puts them into practice is like a wise man who built his house on the rock."*

Storms will come. Winds will blow. But those whose lives are anchored in the Word will stand unshaken. Victory is not the absence of trials but the presence of stability through them. The Word keeps you grounded when feelings fail. It reminds you that God is faithful, even when life feels unfair.

When Job lost everything, he held onto the Word of who God was. *"Though He slay me, yet will I trust Him."* (Job 13:15). That trust was born from revelation. Every trial is a test of whether you will stand on your feelings or on the Word. Feelings fade, but the Word endures forever.

5. The Word as an Agent of Transformation

The ultimate proof that the Word is active in your life is change. God's Word doesn't just inform; it transforms.

Psalm 119:11 says, *"I have hidden your word in my heart that I might not sin against you."* The Word cleanses the heart and shapes the character. Transformation is the highest victory - the victory over self. The Word cuts away pride, fear, bitterness, and sin. It molds you into the likeness of Christ. Every time you submit to the Word, you are winning the battle against the flesh. The more of the Word you absorb, the less room there is for defeat.

The Word is like a mirror (James 1:23-25). It shows you who you truly are - not your flaws, but your potential in Christ. When you see yourself through the mirror of the Word, you stop living as a victim and start walking as a victor.

So how do I use the word for victory?

We have already established the power and importance of the Word of God in a believer's life. The greatest victories you will ever experience will come through the declared Word of God. When the

64

Word fills your heart, your mouth becomes its echo. Then, when trials arise, your default response is no longer fear, but faith; not panic, but proclamation.

To understand how this works, we must see the contrast between God's strategy and Satan's strategy. The Word of God is the believer's absolute truth (Psalm 119:160). This means whatever the Word says you are, you are. Whatever the Word says you have, you have. Whatever the Word says God will do, He will do.

The devil, on the other hand, operates only through lies. Jesus said of him, *"He was a murderer from the beginning... there is no truth in him. When he lies, he speaks his native language."* - John 8:44. Everything Satan does is deception. Even sickness, fear, and lack are extensions of his illusion - attempts to make the believer doubt what God has already declared. The first rule of victory through the Word is this: God's Word is truth; Satan's word is a lie. Therefore, we must invest our time, faith, and focus in knowing and standing upon God's truth.

Contending for the Word

So how do you use the Word for victory? You contend for it.

To contend means to fight, struggle, or hold fast to something of great value. Spiritually, contending means holding onto God's Word in faith until it manifests in your life. It is saying, "I know what God's Word declares about me; even though I don't yet see it, I will not let go until it becomes reality."

Imagine someone who has just received a troubling medical report. The doctor's words are real, but they are not final. God's Word says, *"By His stripes, you are healed."* (Isaiah 53:5). Contending means choosing that truth over the diagnosis - not by denying reality, but by declaring a higher one.

To contend effectively, you must embrace seven biblical postures of faith.

1. Understand That God's Word Is an Invitation, not a Guarantee

When God speaks, it is not an automatic outcome - it is a divine invitation to partnership. His promises reveal His intention, but our faith-filled response activates their manifestation. Every Word from God carries both revelation and responsibility. When you hear a Word, Heaven is inviting you into cooperation - to act, believe, and build according to what God has said.

This is why Paul told Timothy, *"...use the prophecies about you to help you fight well in the Lord's battles."* - 1 Timothy 1:18 (NLT)

God's Word is not a certificate of what will happen automatically - it's an invitation to join Heaven's work on earth. The moment you receive a Word, you've been called into a faith project.

God may declare healing over your life, but that Word requires participation. You partner with it by speaking life instead of fear, stewarding your body wisely, and filling your atmosphere with worship instead of worry. When you meditate on healing Scriptures daily, you are saying, *"Lord, I receive the invitation - let Your Word become flesh in me."*

2. Contend Through Prayer

Prayer is the believer's first and strongest response to the Word. It is where revelation becomes conversation and promise becomes reality. When we pray the Word, we are not reminding God of what

He forgot; we are reminding our hearts of what He has promised. Prayer is where the unseen begins to take form.

God said in Ezekiel 36:37 (NLT), *"I am ready to hear Israel's prayers and to increase their numbers like a flock."* God promised rain to Elijah, yet Elijah still prayed until clouds appeared (1 Kings 18). The Word sets direction for prayer; prayer sets the stage for manifestation.

If the Word says, *"I am the Lord who heals you"* (Exodus 15:26), take that verse to prayer. Say, "Father, Your Word declares You are my Healer. Let that healing flow through every part of my body." Keep praying until peace replaces fear. Prayer turns the written Word into living experience.

3. Contend Through Alignment

The Word of God does not just inform you - it forms you. To align with the Word means to bring your life, thoughts, and behavior into agreement with what God has spoken. The Word cannot work in rebellion. Obedience is the soil in which revelation bears fruit.

When God gives you a promise, He is also revealing the posture required to carry it. Alignment protects what prayer initiates. Habakkuk 2:2-3 (NLT) says, *"Write my answer plainly... though it tarries, wait patiently, for it will surely take place."* Alignment means preparing in faith before you see fulfillment - building Noah's ark before it rains.

If God's Word promises healing, align your lifestyle with His truth. Speak life instead of fear. Release bitterness that poisons the heart. Rest, eat, and care for your body as a temple of the Spirit. Refuse to live stressed and unforgiving. You cannot pray for healing while holding onto habits that harm you. Victory thrives in obedience.

4. Contend by Guarding the Word

Every Word you receive will face opposition. The moment truth is planted, the enemy seeks to uproot it. Jesus explained that the Word can be stolen when the heart is distracted, offended, or doubting (Mark 4:15-19). Guarding the Word means protecting it from contamination - fear, unbelief, and negative voices that contradict what God has said.

"Until the time came to fulfill his dreams, the Lord tested Joseph's character." - Psalm 105:19. Guarding the Word is choosing to believe even when you don't see. It is revisiting, rehearsing, and reinforcing what God has said until it becomes your dominant thought.

After declaring healing, you might feel worse before you feel better. That's not failure; it's a test. When symptoms scream louder, hold the Word tighter. Declare, *"I believe the report of the Lord."* Keep healing Scriptures on your walls, in your phone, and on your tongue. Let the Word saturate your atmosphere until it shifts your reality.

5. Contend Through Patience

Patience is not weakness; it is spiritual maturity in motion. It means trusting God's timing even when your emotions want to rush ahead. God's Word never fails, but it unfolds in appointed seasons. To contend through patience is to wait with faith, not frustration - to worship while waiting.

"God makes everything beautiful for its own time." - Ecclesiastes

3:11

Impatience births Ishmael; patience births Isaac. The delay is never denial - it is preparation. You may pray for healing and still wake up in pain. That doesn't mean God hasn't moved - it means the process is still unfolding. Keep trusting His Word. Take every small improvement as proof of progress. Worship while waiting. Don't give up because it's slow - miracles often start beneath the surface.

Patience keeps you from giving up before the promise arrives.

6. Contend by Staying in the Presence

Victory is sustained by proximity. The power of the Word is strengthened in the presence of the One who spoke it. When you stay near to God, your faith stays alive. The more you commune with Him, the less room fear has to whisper.

"Apart from Me you can do nothing." - John 15:5

Religion performs to impress; relationship abides to receive. Staying in His presence means consistent prayer, worship, and time in the Word - not out of duty, but delight. It's where divine strength renews the human heart.

When fear of sickness rises, don't withdraw - run into His presence. Let worship play in your home. Read healing Scriptures out loud. Sit quietly and listen for His peace. The presence of God has a healing effect; it calms the heart, strengthens the body, and realigns your perspective. Many have found healing simply because they lingered long enough for peace to take over panic.

7. Contend Through Living in Faith and Gratitude

Faith believes it is done; gratitude celebrates as though it's already seen. These two work together to keep your heart expectant and your confession strong. Gratitude prevents frustration and keeps your faith anchored in joy.

"Let us hold tightly without wavering to the hope we affirm, for God can be trusted to keep His promise." - Hebrews 10:23

To live in faith and gratitude is to say, *"I may not see it yet, but I know my God - and He is faithful."* This posture keeps you above circumstances and positions you for manifestation.

Before you see full recovery, begin to thank God. Say, "Lord, thank You that healing is already working in my body." Let gratitude replace complaint. Even if you're taking medicine, do it with faith - believing God is working through every step. Speak life daily: "I'm getting stronger; His healing flows through me."

Faith keeps you focused; gratitude keeps you joyful. Together, they pull the promise from Heaven into earth.

Living the Word Daily

Contending for the Word is not a one-time act; it's a daily lifestyle. It's reading, speaking, and living Scripture until it becomes your reflex. The Word is not just what you quote in crisis - it's what you embody in character.

When the body aches, when reports come, or when fear knocks, remember: you are not helpless; you are armed. The Word in your mouth is the sword in your hand. Keep declaring, keep aligning, keep praying, and keep trusting.

The victory is already written - you simply contend until it's revealed.

The Word and the Spirit

The Holy Spirit and the Word always work together. The Spirit gives life to the Word, and the Word gives clarity to the Spirit. John 6:63 says, *"The words I speak to you are spirit and life."* The Spirit without the Word leads to emotionalism; the Word without the Spirit leads to intellectualism. Victory requires both.

When the Spirit quickens the Word within you, it becomes Rhema. He reminds you of Scriptures at just the right time. He gives you understanding when you read. He turns verses into voices. Many Christians desire power but neglect the Word. Yet, even Jesus, full of the Holy Spirit, quoted Scripture in battle. The Spirit uses the Word as ammunition. The more Word you have, the more weapons the Spirit can use through you.

To live a victorious life, walk daily in the fellowship of the Word and the Spirit. They are Heaven's twin engines for power and direction.

Let's Recap

Victory through the Word means building your life on the unshakable foundation of God's truth. The Logos is the written, eternal Word - the foundation of truth. The Rhema is the spoken, revealed Word - God's specific Word to you for a specific moment. Both are to be obeyed with precision for guaranteed victory. The Word of God is both food and a sword - it feeds your faith and fights your battles.

It renews your mind, transforms your character, and sustains you through trials. When joined with the Holy Spirit, the Word becomes an unstoppable force. Every victory begins with a verse believed, spoken, and lived. When you fill your heart with the Word, the devil can no longer fill your mind with lies.

You do not fight with your feelings; you fight with the Word. For it is written - and what is written cannot be undone.

A Prayer for the Word

Father, thank You for Your Word - living, powerful, and eternal. Teach me to love it, meditate on it, and speak it boldly. Open my eyes to see the treasures hidden within its pages. Fill my heart with the Logos and quicken my spirit with Rhema. May Your Word shape my thoughts, direct my steps, and anchor my faith. Let it be my sword in battle and my bread in peace. In Jesus' mighty name, amen.

CHAPTER

5

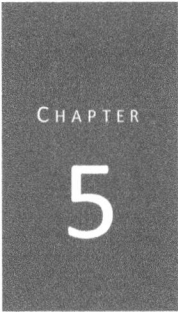

THE PRINCIPLE OF DIVINE AUTHORITY

We ended the previous chapter by understanding that the Word of God is not just information; it is a living force that transforms and establishes victory in the believer's life. But the Word is not meant to stand alone. It carries within it another mystery - a divine authority that authorizes the use of what the Word declares. That authority is found in the Name of Jesus.

There are three inseparable weapons that God has entrusted to His children: His Word, His Name, and His Spirit. The Word reveals His will; the Name enforces it, the Spirit Executes it. The Word establishes your legal right; the Name allows for the legal execution of your heavenly authority through the Spirit of God. When you hold these three in revelation, you live as a believer who cannot be defeated.

"Then Peter said, 'Silver and gold I do not have, but what I do have I give you: In the name of Jesus Christ of Nazareth, rise up and walk.'" - Acts 3:6 (NKJV) When Peter stood before the lame man at the Beautiful Gate, he did not offer him money or sympathy. He offered him what heaven had deposited within him - the Name. And the moment he invoked that Name, divine power was released. The

man who had never walked stood up and began leaping and praising God.

This was not Peter's power; it was not his eloquence or his personal holiness. It was the power of the Name of Jesus - a name given to believers to represent heaven's authority on earth.

The Weight of a Name

In Scripture, a name was never just a label. It carried a person's identity, character, reputation, authority, and influence. A name was a declaration of their nature. That's why God often changed names in the Bible - Abram became Abraham, Jacob became Israel, and Simon became Peter - because their identities were shifting to match God's purpose for them.

A name revealed essence and authority. When David faced Goliath, he said, *"You come to me with a sword, with a spear, and with a javelin, but I come to you in the name of the Lord of hosts, the God of the armies of Israel"* (1 Samuel 17:45). David didn't come in physical strength; he came in covenant authority. The Name he invoked represented everything God was and everything God could do.

In the same way, when you invoke the Name of Jesus, you are not merely repeating syllables. You are stepping into the authority of the Son of God - His essence, His character, His power, and His reputation in heaven, on earth, and under the earth.

"The name of the LORD is a strong tower; the righteous run to it and are safe." - Proverbs 18:10 (NKJV). When you run to that Name, you

are not running to a sound; you are running to a Person - to His power, His protection, and His promise. The Name of the Lord is not a hiding place of fear; it is a fortress of victory. So I ask you today, in whose name do you function?

The Source of the Name

To understand why the Name of Jesus carries such authority, we must understand where that Name comes from.

In Exodus 3:14, when Moses asked God for His name, God replied, "I AM WHO I AM." In Hebrew, that is YHWH (Yahweh) - the self-existent, eternal, all-sufficient One. This was not merely an introduction; it was a revelation of God's nature. God was saying, *"I exist because I am God. I depend on no one. Everything depends on Me."*

Later in Scripture, this eternal name, Yahweh, is coupled with Adonai - which means Lord, Master, and Owner. The title "Adonai" describes dominion and authority, while "Yahweh" reveals eternal being and covenant love. Together, they form the foundation of divine sovereignty.

In the New Testament, the Greek equivalent for "Adonai" is Kyrios, meaning Lord. So when we read that *"every tongue will confess that Jesus Christ is Lord"* (Philippians 2:11), the Bible is declaring that Jesus shares in the full divine authority of Yahweh-Adonai Himself.

This means Jesus is not merely someone who uses God's power; He is that power made flesh. When you say *"in the name of Jesus,"* you are standing in the covenant authority of the eternal God - the same God who said, *"Let there be light,"* and light appeared.

"Therefore God exalted Him to the highest place and gave Him the name that is above every name, that at the name of Jesus every knee should bow, in heaven and on earth and under the earth." - Philippians 2:9-10 (NIV)

Jesus did not receive the Name above all names by default; He received it through obedience. He humbled Himself, lived as a man, and submitted to death - even death on a cross. And because of His obedience, the Father exalted Him and conferred upon Him a Name of supreme authority.

Notice the wording - *"gave Him the name."* The definite article "the" matters. At birth, He was called Jesus (Yeshua), which means "The Lord saves." But after His resurrection and exaltation, He was given the Name - the very authority and dominion of heaven itself.

So when we declare "in the Name of Jesus," we are invoking not only the memory of the Man who walked the earth, but the authority of the risen Lord who reigns at the right hand of God the Father.

This is why demons tremble at that Name (Luke 10:17). This is why sickness responds to that Name (Acts 3:6). This is why salvation is possible only through that Name (Acts 4:12). The Name of Jesus carries the complete weight of divine sovereignty and redemption.

The Difference Between "the Name Jesus" and "the Name of Jesus"

In Peter's time, "Jesus" (Yeshua) was a common Hebrew name. There were other men named Jesus, but none of them carried the Name of Jesus. The difference is in the authority behind the "name of" Jesus. The name is not "Jesus", but that name belongs to Jesus. That name is JHWH Adonai (Kyrios). We will get into that shortly, but all you need to know now is that the power is not in the sound - it is in the One who owns it.

We see this truth illustrated in Acts 19:13-16, where the sons of Sceva attempted to cast out demons using the phrase *"We adjure you by the Jesus whom Paul preaches."* The demon responded, *"Jesus I know, and Paul I know; but who are you?"* and then overpowered them. The result was disastrous, lol. Don't be like them.

Their failure revealed a crucial lesson: While the Name of Jesus carries ultimate authority, it only operates through alignment. God's power flows through order, not rebellion. When you live under His lordship, you are authorized to speak with His authority. But when you live outside of His will, you forfeit that legal right.

The seven sons of Sceva discovered this the hard way. They invoked the Name without submission and were humiliated. To operate effectively in the Name, you must remain submitted to the One who owns it. This is not about perfection; it's about position. The Name doesn't work because we are flawless; it works because we are surrendered. The apostles understood this truth, and they carried the revelation of that Name everywhere they went.

When opposition from the religious rose against them, it's worth noting that the leaders didn't fear their strategies; they feared the power of the Name. *"So, they called them and commanded them not to speak at all nor teach in the name of Jesus."* - Acts 4:18 (NKJV) The Name had become their weapon and their identity. The enemy knew that as long as they used it, they could not be stopped.

And what did the apostles do? They went back to their company and prayed, *"Lord, look upon their threats and grant to Your servants that with all boldness they may speak Your word, by stretching out Your hand to heal, and that signs and wonders may be done through the name of Your holy Servant Jesus."* - Acts 4:29–30 (NKJV) They did not ask for the persecution to end; they asked for greater boldness to use the Name. That is the posture of faith - not retreat, but release.

And Scripture records that *"the place where they were assembled was shaken, and they were all filled with the Holy Spirit."* (Acts 4:31). Heaven responded to their prayer because it was prayed in alignment with divine authority and purpose.

All this teaches us that the Name of Jesus is not a formula; it is a relationship. You cannot use the Name if you are not under the authority of the One who owns it. The sons of Sceva tried to use a label without legal right - and the spiritual world recognized the difference.

The power of the Name flows not from pronunciation but from position - the believer's position in Christ. When you belong to Him, His Name belongs to you. When you are under His Lordship, His authority flows through you.

That's why Jesus said, *"Behold, I give you authority to trample on serpents and scorpions, and over all the power of the enemy, and nothing shall by any means hurt you."* - Luke 10:19 (NKJV). When you stand under His authority, you operate in His authority. The Name of Jesus becomes more than words - it becomes your right to victory.

The Authority of the Name

Authority, by definition, is delegated power. It means you have permission to act on behalf of another.

When a police officer stops traffic, he doesn't do so by physical strength but by the authority vested in him by the government he represents. His badge tells everyone that behind his raised hand stands an entire legal system. A police officer doesn't fight criminals with personal strength but with the authority of the law. The power behind his badge is not in his muscles but in the government he represents.

In the same way, the believer's power does not rest in emotion or volume; it rests in legal authority. When you stand in the Name of Jesus, heaven recognizes your command because it recognizes the office you hold in Christ.

"Truly, I tell you, whatever you bind on earth will be bound in heaven, and whatever you loose on earth will be loosed in heaven." - Matthew 18:18 (NIV). Binding and loosing are legal terms. To bind means to restrict or forbid. To loose means to release or permit. These are judicial actions - and the Name of Jesus is the signature that authorizes them. Angels move at His command (Psalm 103:20). Demons tremble at His authority (Luke 10:17). Creation responds to His lordship (Mark 4:39-41).

So, from now on, I need you to know that when you pray, speak, or command in the Name of Jesus, you are acting as His legal representative on earth. You are backed by the legal system of heaven, just like the police. I need you to know that when you pray "in the Name of Jesus," you are not informing heaven of your need; you are executing a heavenly decree. You are using divine jurisdiction to enforce God's will on earth. The Father responds not merely to your words but to your position - your standing in the Son. The spiritual world recognizes this, too.

"And whatever you do in word or deed, do all in the name of the Lord Jesus, giving thanks to God the Father through Him." - Colossians 3:17 (NKJV). Notice the phrase "whatever you do." This means the Name of Jesus is not limited to church services or prayer meetings. It extends into your workplace, your family, your health, and every dimension of life. Every action taken in His Name becomes an opportunity for heaven to manifest on earth.

When you understand that the Name of Jesus is both your authority and your identity, you stop fighting battles in your strength. You stop pleading for what has already been paid for. You stop asking the enemy to leave; you command him to go.

When an ambassador speaks, he does not speak for himself; he speaks for his government. His voice carries the weight of the one who sent him. The Bible says, *"We are ambassadors for Christ, as though God were making His appeal through us."* - 2 Corinthians 5:20 (NIV)

To speak in Jesus' Name is to function as His ambassador. God recognizes your words as His words when you speak in alignment with His will. Demons, sickness, and circumstances know this and recognize it too. That's why Peter could boldly say, *"Such as I have, give I thee."* He knew that what he carried - the Name of Jesus - was heaven's currency for transformation.

Child of God, that same Name has been entrusted to you. That Name works as powerfully today as it did at the Beautiful Gate. You don't need a new authority; you need a new awareness.

So you now have the name, but what does it mean for your victory? As a believer, here are a few things you need to know about this name in relation to your victory:

1. The Name Is Your Access

The Name of Jesus does not only represent authority; it also grants access. It is the key that unlocks heaven's resources. Jesus said, *"Whatever you ask the Father in My name He will give you"* (John 16:23). Notice that He didn't say "whatever you ask Me," but "the Father." The Name of Jesus gives you the right of entry into the throne room of grace. You don't come as a stranger or a beggar; you come as a son.

When you say, "Father, in the Name of Jesus," heaven's doors swing open. Angels recognize it. Demons retreat from it. The Father honors it - because that Name represents His beloved Son. The Name of Jesus is your access card to divine provision, healing, peace, and victory. Every promise of God is yes and amen in Him (2 Corinthians 1:20). The question is not whether the Name works - it is whether you will use it with revelation and believe it actually works.

Everything heaven has to offer is distributed through that Name. The Name is the believer's signature of inheritance - the seal that guarantees every promise.

2. The Name Is Your Victory

When you invoke the Name of Jesus with belief and understanding, you bring heaven's government into earthly situations. The sick are healed, the bound are freed, the oppressed are delivered, and the impossible becomes possible.

The Name of Jesus works! It works because it is rooted in His finished work, His exaltation, and His present reign. His Finished Work - The cross established Jesus as Redeemer. He conquered sin, death, and the grave (Colossians 2:15). The Name carries that victory. When you speak it, you remind hell of its defeat. His Exaltation - After resurrection, the Father gave Him supreme authority (Philippians 2:9-11). The Name carries that authority. When you invoke it, you represent His rule. His Present Reign - Jesus now sits at the right hand of the Father, interceding for us (Romans 8:34). The Name carries that intercession. When you pray in His Name, you align with His ongoing ministry.

When these truths live in your spirit, the Name of Jesus becomes more than a word - it becomes a guaranteed victory strategy for you as a child of God. Scripture declares, *"At the name of Jesus every knee should bow, in heaven and on earth and under the earth."* (Philippians 2:10). Therefore, very knee - spiritual or physical - must respond to the authority of that Name.

It's not your loudness that makes demons flee; it's your legal right in Christ. It's not your fasting that heals the sick; it's your faith in His finished work. The Name is the believer's badge of authority. The power has already been granted; it is now to be exercised.

"And His name, through faith in His name, has made this man strong." - Acts 3:16 (NKJV) When you begin to walk in the revelation of that Name, you realize that victory is no longer something you pursue; it's something you enforce.

3. The Name Is Your Lifestyle

"And whatever you do, in word or deed, do everything in the name of the Lord Jesus, giving thanks to God the Father through him." -

Colossians 3:17 (ESV)

When Jesus gave us His Name, He didn't intend for us to use it as a closing line for prayers. I know I am guilty of this too. I have used the name of Jesus as a filler line in my prayers while I think about what to say next. This became a habit I struggled to break for a while. I found myself saying "in the name of Jesus" not because I meant to say it and with revelation, but because I was just used to saying it while I fix my words.

But Jesus gave us this name for us to live by it. The early believers understood this truth in a way that many in our generation have forgotten. They did not use the Name as an expression of ritual but as a revelation of identity. They lived, spoke, healed, preached, and even suffered in the Name.

Every miracle they performed, every prayer they prayed, and every persecution they endured was directly linked to that Name. To be a Christian in the book of Acts was to be a carrier of the Name. The first believers were birthed through the power of that Name. On the day of Pentecost, Peter declared, *"Repent, and let every one of you be baptized in the name of Jesus Christ for the remission of sins"* (Acts 2:38). That day, three thousand souls were saved - all under the banner of that Name.

The Name was their foundation of salvation. It represented forgiveness, new birth, and covenant belonging. Baptism in the Name wasn't a ritual; it was a declaration of ownership. It meant, "I now belong to Christ; His Name marks me." *"Salvation is found in no one else, for there is no other name under heaven given to mankind by which we must be saved."* - Acts 4:12 (NIV)

The Name of Jesus became the only doorway into the kingdom of God. Every person who came into covenant did so through that Name. That is still true today - no one can come to the Father except through Him (John 14:6).

4. The Name Is Your Identity

We have already covered Identity in chapter 2. However, In Acts 11:26, we read that *"the disciples were first called Christians in Antioch."* The word Christian literally means "little Christ." It wasn't initially a compliment; it was a label of mockery - but it became their highest honor.

To be called a Christian meant to carry Christ's identity, His nature, and His authority. It meant that when people saw them, they saw Jesus. They spoke like Him, loved like Him, and performed miracles in His Name. They were living proof that Christ's presence did not end with His ascension; it continued through His people.

The early church understood that the Name of Jesus wasn't just given for confession - it was given for representation. They represented Christ wherever they went. When Peter and John healed the lame man, they didn't say, *"By our holiness, be healed."* They said, *"In the name of Jesus Christ of Nazareth, rise up and walk."* (Acts 3:6).

This is why the world marveled at them. They recognized that these men were ordinary but carried something extraordinary - the authority of another world. *"When they saw the courage of Peter and John and realized that they were unschooled, ordinary men, they were astonished and took note that these men had been with Jesus."* - Acts 4:13 (NIV)

The early church understood that to carry the Name means more than using it occasionally; it means making it your lifestyle. And so it should be for you today: **Speak in the Name**: Let every word you speak carry the fragrance of Christ's character. **Pray in the Name:** Approach the Father confidently, knowing He hears the Son in you. **Serve in the Name**: Whatever you do, do it as unto the Lord, not for applause. Suffer in the Name: When opposition arises because of your faith, count it joy that you are worthy to bear His Name (Acts 5:41).

To live in the Name is to live with divine consciousness - aware that heaven's authority resides in you, not because of who you are, but because of Whose you are. That is what it means to operate in the Name: to live in such fellowship with Jesus that His presence becomes unmistakable upon you.

5. The Name Is Your Heavenly Passport

Before His ascension, Jesus gave His disciples a clear mandate: *"Go therefore and make disciples of all nations, baptizing them in the name of the Father and of the Son and of the Holy Spirit."* - Matthew 28:19 (ESV)

This commission was not given to a few apostles; it was given to every believer. The call to "go" is inseparable from the call to "represent." You cannot go in your own strength; you go in the Name (Passport). That Name is your passport into the nations, your defense against evil, your authority in prayer, and your banner in warfare. It is both your introduction and your conclusion. Every work you do for God, every act of ministry, every prayer you pray - must begin and end there.

When Jesus said, *"These signs will accompany those who believe: In*

My Name they will cast out demons..." (Mark 16:17), He was not describing a special class of Christians; He was describing every believer who walks in faith and understanding. The same power that worked through Peter and Paul works through you today - not because you are extraordinary, but because the Name you bear is.

When you pray, heaven moves. When you declare, demons flee. When you stand in faith, circumstances shift - not because of emotional intensity, but because of divine identity. The entire spiritual world recognizes rank, and the believer who carries revelation of the Name outranks every demonic principality. You don't need to fight harder; you need to speak wiser. You don't need to shout louder; you need to believe deeper. When you say, "In the Name of Jesus," you are commanding from a position of victory, not desperation.

So, every time you step into prayer, work, ministry, or conflict, remind yourself of this: You carry the Name. It is written on your heart, sealed by the Spirit, and recognized in the heavens. Live worthy of that Name. Speak with the weight of that Name. Walk in the victory of that Name. *"And whatever you do, in word or deed, do everything in the name of the Lord Jesus."* - Colossians 3:17 (NIV)

How to Use the Name

"And His name, through faith in His name, has made this man strong, whom you see and know." - Acts 3:16 (NKJV)

Revelation without application leads to frustration. Many believers know that there is power in the Name of Jesus, but few truly understand how to use it. We can quote the verses and even sing about the Name, but until we learn to apply it with faith and understanding, the power within that Name remains dormant in our lives.

The early church did not just revere the Name - they used it. They invoked it with faith, walked in it with humility, and aligned their actions with heaven's purpose. As a result, the same miracles that Jesus performed continued through them.

Child of God, this same authority belongs to you. You have the legal right and spiritual responsibility to use the Name of Jesus in every area of life. The question is not whether the Name works; the question is whether you know how to work the Name. Using the Name of Jesus effectively requires four key postures of the heart - Faith, Alignment, Relationship, and Humility with Purpose. Let's explore each one carefully.

1. The Name Requires Faith - Not Incantation

Notice that Peter did not simply say, *"His name has made this man strong." He said, "His name, through faith in His name."* The Name alone is powerful, but faith is the key that releases that power.

Faith is not mental agreement; it is spiritual confidence born out of revelation. Peter wasn't experimenting with the Name; *he knew it would work.* His faith was not in his voice or ability but in the authority of the One who sent him.

The same is true for you. When you stand in front of sickness, opposition, or lack, you don't have to beg God for intervention - you speak from the authority already granted to you. Faith makes the unseen realm respond to the revealed will of God. When Peter lifted the lame man at the Beautiful Gate, he didn't recite a formula. He acted on revelation. His faith in the Name made the man strong.

Faith is not saying the right words louder; it's trusting the right Person deeper. The Name of Jesus is not a charm or a spell; it is a covenant weapon that operates by faith in the One who gave it. In Acts 19:13-16, the seven sons of Sceva tried to cast out demons by saying, *"We adjure you by the Jesus whom Paul preaches."* They had learned the words but not the relationship. The demon's response was chilling: *"Jesus I know, and Paul I know; but who are you?"* They were beaten and shamed because they tried to use faith's language without faith's foundation.

You see, faith is not memorized; it is cultivated. It grows through intimacy with God's Word and trust in His nature. When you believe in the One behind the Name, the Name becomes a force in your hands.

"This is the victory that has overcome the world - our faith." - 1 John 5:4 (NKJV) When you use the Name of Jesus, speak with faith. Don't try to sound powerful - be persuaded. Don't command with fear in your heart - command with conviction in your spirit. Faith makes you fearless, and fearless faith moves mountains.

When faced with sickness, don't plead, "Lord, if it's Your will, please heal me." Instead, declare what you already know: "By His stripes I am healed. In the Name of Jesus Christ, body, align with the Word of God." That is not arrogance - it's agreement with truth.

Faith gives the Name its voice. The more you know the Word, the stronger your faith in the Name becomes. You cannot separate the two. The Word informs you; the Name enforces it.

2. The Name Requires Alignment with God's Will

"Now this is the confidence that we have in Him, that if we ask

anything according to His will, He hears us." - 1 John 5:14 (NKJV)

The power of the Name is never for personal ambition; it is for divine purpose. God's Name cannot be attached to anything that contradicts His nature or His plan.

We often ask God to bless what we've chosen, instead of choosing what He's already blessed. Alignment means surrendering your will to His - letting His purpose become your pursuit. When your heart is aligned with His Word, the Name of Jesus becomes unstoppable in your mouth. Jesus Himself modeled this: *"I do not seek My own will, but the will of the Father who sent Me."* (John 5:30). Because He lived in perfect alignment, His every word carried weight. When He spoke to storms, demons, or sickness, they obeyed immediately because He never acted outside the Father's will.

When you pray or declare in the Name of Jesus, pause and ask, "Does this align with His heart? Does this glorify the Father?" If it doesn't, the authority won't flow. The Name operates where the will of God is honored.

Imagine commanding prosperity while neglecting obedience in stewardship - the command may sound right, but it's misaligned. Yet when your finances serve His kingdom, when your generosity mirrors His heart, every declaration you make in His Name over your resources carries heaven's backing.

Alignment gives power direction. Without it, authority is wasted energy.

3. The Name Requires Relationship

"If you abide in Me, and My words abide in you, you will ask what

you desire, and it shall be done for you." - John 15:7 (NKJV) Power without relationship is dangerous. The Name of Jesus is not licensed to strangers; it is entrusted to sons and daughters. The more intimate your walk with Him, the more effectively His Name operates through you.

Peter could say, *"In the Name of Jesus Christ, rise up and walk,"* because he had walked with Jesus. He had seen Him heal, deliver, and raise the dead. He had heard His voice, touched His hands, and received His Spirit. The Name wasn't a theory to Peter; it was his lived reality.

When Jesus said, *"I am the vine, you are the branches,"* He was teaching that spiritual authority flows through connection. A branch doesn't bear fruit by trying harder; it bears fruit by staying connected.

Faith gets you access, but relationship keeps the flow. If you want consistent power in the Name, stay close to the One who gave it.

That's why Jesus taught, *"Whatever we ask we receive from Him, because we keep His commandments and do those things that are pleasing in His sight."* - 1 John 3:22 (NKJV)

A disobedient life cannot carry obedient authority. You can't resist God in private and expect the devil to obey you in public. Authority flows through fellowship and submission. When you face a stubborn situation - whether emotional oppression, fear, or temptation - don't only use the Name as a command; use it as communion. Say, "Jesus, I know You are here with me. I lean into Your presence. I draw on Your strength." That is relationship. From that place of intimacy, you then speak with boldness: "In the Name of Jesus Christ, I refuse this fear. Peace, reign in my heart."

The more you know Him, the more natural His Name flows through you. Relationships give the Name its confidence.

4. The Name Requires Humility and Purpose

"God resists the proud, but gives grace to the humble." - James 4:6 (NKJV) Humility and divine purpose are like the twin engines that keep spiritual authority steady. The power of the Name is not given to exalt man but to glorify God. Whenever pride, self-promotion, or personal agendas creep in, the anointing is restrained.

Jesus modeled humility perfectly. He had the power to command legions of angels, yet He chose servanthood. *"The Son of Man did not come to be served, but to serve."* (Matthew 20:28). Because His motives were pure, His words carried weight. When God can trust your heart, He will trust you with power. The Name of Jesus must always be used to fulfill heaven's agenda - to bring salvation, healing, restoration, and glory to God.

In Acts 3, after the healing of the lame man, Peter immediately redirected attention from himself: *"Why look so intently at us, as though by our own power or godliness we had made this man walk? ... It is His Name, through faith in His Name, that has made this man strong."* (Acts 3:12,16). That is humility. Peter understood he was only a vessel. The moment you start taking credit for what the Name does, you begin to lose the flow of that power.

If you pray for someone and they are healed, don't say, "God used me mightily." Instead, say, "Jesus healed them." That statement alone keeps your heart pure and the channel open. The more you give Him glory, the more He entrusts you with grace. Humility and divine purpose keep the Name untarnished in your mouth. You are not using the Name for personal fame; you are carrying it as a sacred trust to reveal God's love to the world.

Putting It All Together

To operate fully in the authority of the Name: Know the Word - Build your faith in what the Name represents. Check your Alignment - Make sure your desire matches His will. Cultivate Relationship - Abide in His presence and obey His Word. Stay Humble and Purposeful - Let every act glorify Jesus, not yourself.

Now, take these truths beyond theory. Use them. When sickness arises: Speak to it - "In the Name of Jesus Christ, I command healing in this body. I speak restoration by the power of His Word." When fear or anxiety attacks: Declare - "In the Name of Jesus, I reject the spirit of fear. The peace of Christ rules in my heart."

When provision seems distant: Pray - "Father, in the Name of Jesus, I thank You that all my needs are met according to Your riches in glory. I refuse lack, and I walk in divine provision." When facing demonic opposition: Stand firm - "In the Name of Jesus Christ, I command every dark power assigned against my family to bow and depart."

The Name of Jesus is not bound by circumstance or geography. It works in hospitals, homes, offices, and battlefields. Wherever faith is present, that Name performs.

Guard the Name just as a soldier maintains his weapon. You must guard the integrity of the Name in your life. That means refusing to speak it in vain or use it carelessly. Do not use the Name as filler or tradition - use it with reverence. Do not attach the Name to disobedient plans - seek alignment first. Do not let pride taint your use of the Name - give glory to the Lord.

The Name of Jesus is heaven's greatest trust in your hands. Treat it as holy. Speak it with conviction. Protect it with your character. Living in the Victory of the Name. To live in the victory of the Name is to live in continuous awareness that Jesus has already triumphed. When He rose from the grave, He stripped every principality and power of their dominion (Colossians 2:15). He made a public spectacle of them, and then He handed the keys of authority to you. Yes! To you!

When you understand this, prayer becomes less of a plea and more of an enforcement. You don't beg for victory - you declare it. You don't chase breakthroughs - you release them. Every battle you face is already won in the Name of Jesus. Your part is to enforce the victory through faith-filled words and Spirit-led action.

Let's Recap

Victory through the Name is one of Heaven's greatest principles for the believer. In the Old Testament, God revealed Himself as YHWH - "I AM."

Through His covenant names, He showed His nature as Provider, Healer, Peace, and Righteousness. In Jesus, all those revelations are fulfilled. He is the complete expression of YHWH - now revealed as Kurios, the Lord of all. The Name of Jesus carries full authority over every power, disease, and circumstance. The Name works through faith, relationship, and submission, not mere repetition. When you live, pray, and act in His Name, you operate under Heaven's backing.

The Name of Jesus is both a weapon in warfare and a covering in peace. It carries His presence, His victory, and His identity within it. When you call His Name, Heaven responds. When you speak His Name, demons bow. When you live in His Name, victory becomes your nature. The Name of Jesus is not simply what you say - it is who you represent. You bear His mark, you speak His authority, and you live His victory.

A Prayer of Surrender and Victory

Father, thank You for the power in the Name of Jesus. I honor that holy Name - the Name above every name. Teach me to live, speak, and walk under its authority. Forgive me for every time I have taken that Name lightly. Today, I choose to exalt Jesus as Lord over every area of my life - my family, my mind, my health, my future, and my calling. I lift up His Name over every battle and declare that victory belongs to the Lord. May my life continually glorify that matchless Name - Jesus, my Savior, my Banner, and my King. Amen.

THE PRINCIPLE OF COVENANT

"And they overcame him by the blood of the Lamb and by the word of their testimony, and they did not love their lives to the death." - Revelation 12:11

If the Name of Jesus is the believer's authority, then the Blood of Jesus is the believer's assurance. The Blood is the seal of every promise, the foundation of every victory, and the heart of the gospel itself. Without the Blood, there is no redemption, no forgiveness, no covenant, and no access to God and definitely no Victory.

Throughout Scripture, victory is always connected to blood. The first altar ever built was sealed with blood; the first covenant ever made was confirmed by blood; and the first Passover deliverance was secured through blood on a doorpost. From Genesis to Revelation, the story of redemption flows in one connected thread - from the lamb slain for Adam's covering to the Lamb slain for the sins of the world.

The Blood of Jesus is not symbolic poetry; it is spiritual power. It carries **divine life**, for *"the life of the flesh is in the blood"* (Leviticus

17:11). The Blood of Jesus represents the very life of God released on our behalf. When you understand the mystery of the Blood, you understand the mystery of victory.

The Necessity of the Blood

From the beginning, God established a principle: sin demands payment, and the payment is blood. Romans 6:23 says, *"The wages of sin is death."* When Adam and Eve sinned, something innocent had to die so that the guilty might live. Scripture tells us that God clothed them with garments of skin (Genesis 3:21) - the first recorded death in the Bible. Blood had to be shed for their shame to be covered.

That principle became the foundation of the sacrificial system. Hebrews 9:22 declares, *"Without the shedding of blood there is no forgiveness."* Every offering brought to the altar was a substitute, a temporary atonement until the perfect sacrifice would come. The Blood speaks of exchange - life for life. It declares that death has been paid in full. Every time Israel sacrificed a lamb, they were prophetically declaring that one day, a greater Lamb would come - One whose Blood would not merely cover sin but remove it forever.

From the garden to Calvary's hill, God was preparing humanity to understand one truth: victory is found through the Blood.

The Blood In The Covenant

The Bible is a book of covenants - divine agreements sealed with blood. A covenant is not a contract; it is a sacred bond of life and death.

When God made a covenant with Abraham in Genesis 15, animals were cut in half, and a smoking firepot (symbolizing God's presence) passed between the pieces. The blood from the animals showed that this promise was serious and could never be broken.

In Exodus 24, Moses sprinkled blood on the altar and on the people, saying, *"This is the blood of the covenant that the Lord has made with you."* It symbolized that Israel now belonged to God - redeemed, set apart, and covered.

In ancient times, two parties in a blood covenant would mix their blood, signifying shared identity. They would exchange names, resources, and strength. If one was attacked, the other was obligated to defend.

This imagery becomes breathtaking when you realize that through Jesus, God entered into covenant with humanity. His Blood became the eternal seal of divine partnership. Now, when Satan comes against you, he is not only confronting you - he is confronting the covenant between God and His Son. You are not fighting alone; you are backed by covenant blood.

The night before Israel's deliverance from Egypt, God instructed them to sacrifice a spotless lamb and apply its blood on their doorposts (Exodus 12). He said, *"When I see the blood, I will pass over you."* That night, death swept through Egypt, but wherever the blood was found, safety was invoked. It wasn't about who was inside the house - rich or poor, young or old - it was about whether the blood was present. The blood became their victory.

This was not superstition; it was substitution. The lamb took the place of the firstborn. The blood declared, "Judgment has already fallen here." Centuries later, John the Baptist looked at Jesus and cried out, *"Behold, the Lamb of God who takes away the sin of the world!"* (John 1:29). The Passover was pointing to Him all along.

Just as Israel was delivered from Pharaoh through the blood of a lamb, we are delivered from sin, Satan, death and all dark powers through the Blood of Christ. On the cross, Jesus became the ultimate Passover Lamb. His Blood was not spilled accidentally; it was offered intentionally. Every drop carried divine purpose.

As He hung there, heaven and earth witnessed the greatest exchange in history. Sin was judged, justice was satisfied, and mercy was released. The Lamb of God took our place, bearing our guilt and shame so that we could bear His righteousness. When Jesus cried, *"It is finished!"* (John 19:30), He was declaring that the debt was paid - not partially, but completely.

Hebrews 9:12 says, *"He entered once for all into the Holy Place, not by the blood of goats and calves but by His own blood, thus obtaining eternal redemption."* Unlike the blood of animals that had to be offered repeatedly, the Blood of Jesus speaks eternally. It does not fade, dry, or lose potency. It forever testifies that sin has been **defeated** and Satan has been **disarmed**.

The Blood of Jesus was not offered on an earthly altar but in Heaven itself. Hebrews 12:24 says His Blood *"speaks a better word than the blood of Abel."* Abel's blood cried out for vengeance; Jesus' Blood cries out for mercy.

The Power in the Blood

The Blood of Jesus accomplishes more than most believers realize. It is not just a symbol of forgiveness - it is a multi-dimensional source of divine victory. The blood speaks to bloodlines. There are things tied to our earthly bloodlines that according to spiritual laws, we must be punished, attacked, suffer, or even destroyed for. BUT! The blood of Jesus cancels them out for our victory's sake. Scripture reveals that the Blood does at least seven powerful things:

1. The blood Redeems

Through the blood of Jesus, you have been redeemed, bought back and set free from the power of sin and Satan. Please understand this: Redemption means that your life is no longer under the ownership of darkness, and no dark forces have a legal claim on you. The enemy cannot lay claim to what Jesus has already paid for in full.

Many people live in cycles of guilt, fear, and addiction because they do not understand the value of this redemption. The blood of Jesus has broken every legal right the enemy once had over your life. You are no longer a slave to sin, to your past, or to any generational curse. Your bloodline is now Jesus Christ.

This means you can walk in freedom every day. When temptation tries to pull you back, declare, "I am redeemed by the blood of Jesus." When guilt whispers that you are not worthy, remind yourself that redemption was not earned, it was purchased. Jesus paid your ransom; you belong to Him. The blood gives you authority to reject the lies of bondage and live as one who has truly been set free.

This means, no matter the situation you find yourself in right now, by virtue of you being redeemed, no longer has a legal right over you, all is redeemed by the blood of Jesus. Health? Redeemed! Depression? Redeemed! Finances? Redeemed!

2. The blood Justifies

Justification means that the blood of Jesus declares you "not guilty." Because of the cross, God now sees you as righteous, clean, and accepted. Romans 5:9 says, *"Being now justified by His blood, we shall be saved from wrath."* You are not trying to earn God's approval; you already have it through Christ. The moment you receive Jesus, His blood erases the record of your wrongs and writes your name in righteousness.

This truth is peace to every believer who has ever struggled with condemnation. The enemy thrives on accusation, but the blood silences his case. When shame tries to replay your past, you can boldly respond, "I have been justified by the blood." Practically, justification means you can approach God with confidence, pray without fear, and live without the weight of guilt. The blood has removed the barrier; you are free to live forgiven.

If the blood already declared you "not guilty", there is no need for you to suffer sickness, no need for bloodline poverty or suffering. Jesus' bloodline is now your bloodline, and that bloodline I rich and healthy.

3. The blood Sanctifies

Sanctification means being set apart for God's holy purpose. Hebrews 13:12 tells us, *"Jesus also suffered... to sanctify the people through His own blood."* The blood of Jesus not only saves you but also separates you from what used to define you. It pulls you out of worldly patterns and dedicates you to divine purpose. You are no longer ordinary-you are consecrated for kingdom use.

This means your desires begin to change. The things you used to chase no longer satisfy. The Holy Spirit, working through the power of the blood, transforms your priorities, your relationships, and even your goals. Sanctification is a process, not a moment, it's walking daily in the awareness that your life belongs to God. Every time you yield to His will, the blood is actively setting you apart for victory.

Therefore, no family bloodline curses, bondages, and rituals have a legal hold on your destiny. Your entire destiny now belongs to God's plans and will.

4. The blood Cleanses

The blood of Jesus does more than cover sin, it cleanses it. 1 John 1:7 declares, *"The blood of Jesus cleanses us from all sin."* This cleansing goes deeper than outward change; it washes the conscience. Many people carry invisible stains, memories, regrets, and failures that haunt them. The blood reaches those hidden places and removes the residue of shame. It purifies you until you can stand before God without fear or guilt.

This means you no longer have to be defined by what happened yesterday. The blood cleanses your story and gives you a new one. Each time you repent and apply the truth of the cross, cleansing flows afresh. You can wake up every morning knowing you are clean, whole, and free to begin again. Victory is not perfection; it's walking daily in the cleansing power of His blood.

5. The blood Protects

We live in a time where there is intense spiritual activity, much of it not of God. Attacks come in ways we never expect: anxiety to steal our peace, distractions to rob our focus, sickness to drain our strength. But the blood of Jesus is our protection, our Passover covering. Just as the Israelites were shielded when the destroyer passed through Egypt, so the believer today is covered under the blood.

This protection is not symbolic, it is spiritual reality. When you pray over your family, your home, or your work and declare the blood of Jesus, you are drawing a divine boundary that darkness cannot cross. Fear loses power when you know you are covered. You don't have to live in paranoia; live in peace. The blood of Jesus is stronger than any curse, darker than any night, and greater than any enemy.

True victory will always be experienced by those who make it a lifestyle to plead the blood of Jesus over everything pertaining their lives, nothing left to chance.

6. The blood Grants Access

Before the cross, only the high priest could enter the Holy of Holies once a year, and only with blood. But Hebrews 10:19 declares, *"We have confidence to enter the Most Holy Place by the blood of Jesus."* The blood tore the veil that separated humanity from God. Now, every believer has 24/7 access to the throne of grace. You don't need a mediator, a title, or a special ritual-the blood is your invitation.

This means you can come to God just as you are, any time, anywhere. When you feel unworthy to pray, remember that access was purchased by blood, not behavior. You don't knock at Heaven's door as a stranger-you walk in as a child. The blood grants you direct communication with your Father. You no longer live distant or disconnected; you live in fellowship and friendship with God. That is victory, living with open access to His presence.

7. The blood Overcomes

Revelation 12:11 declares, *"They overcame him by the blood of the Lamb and by the word of their testimony."* The blood of Jesus is not only a symbol, it is a weapon. It defeats accusations, breaks oppression, and silences every voice of condemnation from the evil one. When Satan reminds you of your failures, the blood reminds him of his defeat.

This means you can stand firm in trials without fear. The blood empowers you to overcome sin, fear, and spiritual attack. When anxiety rises, declare, "The blood of Jesus speaks for me." When you feel unworthy, remember, the blood still works! It allows you to appear before God and stand as worthy, without blame. If that weren't the case, you wouldn't be able to stand before Him. Victory is not about what you can do, it's about what has already been done. The blood is your victory anthem, and every time you apply it in faith, darkness loses its grip.

The Blood of Jesus is Heaven's ultimate weapon against hell's strategies. Scripture says, *"We are not ignorant of the enemy's devices."* (2 Corinthians 2:11). The devil's strategies haven't changed, but his methods adapt to each generation. Let's look at some of the dark works of the enemy that are especially active today, not to glorify him, but to expose him so that you can walk in discernment and victory:

Deception and Confusion of Truth

The blood of Jesus exposes lies and restores clarity to the believer's heart. When Jesus shed His blood, He sealed the covenant of truth between God and man. The same blood that redeemed you now empowers you to discern truth from deception. The enemy thrives where there is ignorance, but the blood brings revelation light that darkness cannot resist. When you plead the blood of Jesus over your mind, confusion breaks. When you study the Word through the lens of the cross, falsehood loses its hold. The blood renews your spiritual sight, helping you see what is of God and what is counterfeit.

Identity Crisis

The blood of Jesus restores identity because it marks you as God's own. When you understand that you were purchased at the highest price, insecurity and confusion lose their grip. You are not what the world labels you; you are who the blood declares you to be: redeemed, chosen, and accepted. When you feel lost, remind yourself that Heaven recognizes you through the blood. It speaks a better word over your life than every lie spoken against you. The blood gives you confidence to say, "I know who I am in Christ," even when the world tries to tell you otherwise.

Perversion and Moral Corruption

The blood of Jesus purifies. It doesn't just forgive the sin of impurity; it cleanses the stain it leaves behind. When a believer applies the blood through repentance, shame loses its authority. The blood breaks the power of lust and resets the heart toward holiness. It gives strength to walk away from what once enslaved you. Every time temptation whispers, you can stand boldly and say, "The blood of Jesus has set me free." The more you meditate on what He accomplished at the cross, the more your desires are sanctified. Purity is not perfection, it's living covered, cleansed, and empowered by the blood.

Distraction and Spiritual Apathy

The blood of Jesus awakens passion and restores spiritual hunger. It draws us back to intimacy with God. When life's noise pulls you in every direction, the blood reminds you of the price of your redemption, and that remembrance rekindles focus. The same blood that opened Heaven's veil invites you to communion with the Father. When you come under its covering, prayer becomes a delight, not a duty. The blood realigns priorities and ignites devotion. It silences worldly noise so you can hear the Spirit's whisper again.

Fear and Anxiety

The blood of Jesus silences fear because it is proof that you are eternally secure. Fear feeds on uncertainty, but the blood guarantees victory. When the Israelites saw the blood on their doorposts, death passed over them, that same Passover power protects you today. Whenever anxiety rises, speak the blood over your mind and atmosphere. It declares, "You are safe, you are loved, you are covered." The blood of Jesus is your assurance that no evil can touch you without God's permission. Faith grows where the blood is honored, and fear flees where the blood is applied.

Rebellion and Pride

The blood of Jesus humbles the heart. It reminds us that victory is not earned but given. Pride dies in the presence of the cross, because the blood declares that we are nothing without grace. Rebellion began in heaven through Lucifer's pride, but the blood broke its curse on earth. When you stay mindful of the blood, humility becomes your nature. The blood teaches submission, to God, to His Word, and to His will. It changes independence into dependence on divine power. True strength is not defiance; it is surrender under the covering of the blood.

Witchcraft and Occult Practices

The blood of Jesus is the ultimate power that defeats every dark spirit and counterfeit miracle. No charm, spell, or ritual can stand against it. At Calvary, Jesus disarmed principalities and powers, making a public spectacle of them. When you declare the blood, you invoke Heaven's highest authority. It covers your home, your dreams, and your destiny. The blood destroys every curse and nullifies every incantation. Darkness can imitate light but cannot overcome the power of the cross. When you stay under the blood, you walk in dominion that no demonic system can touch.

Division and Offense

The blood of Jesus unites what the enemy tries to divide. The cross reconciled man to God and man to man. When you live conscious of the blood, you refuse to carry offense because you remember how much you've been forgiven. The blood dismantles pride and softens the heart toward reconciliation. When conflict arises, pleading the blood over the situation releases peace. The same blood that healed your relationship with God can heal broken friendships, families, and churches. Unity is impossible without forgiveness, and forgiveness flows freely through the blood.

Hopelessness and Depression

The blood of Jesus breathes life into the weary soul. It is Heaven's reminder that you are loved, seen, and not forgotten. Depression thrives where people feel worthless, but the blood declares infinite worth - Jesus deemed you valuable enough to die for. When hopelessness whispers that it's over, the blood proclaims, "It is finished." That means despair is defeated, and new beginnings are possible. Applying the blood through worship and gratitude restores joy. The blood of Jesus is hope in liquid form - it revives what pain tried to bury.

False Light and Self-Deification

The blood of Jesus exposes counterfeit spirituality. The cross stands as proof that man cannot save himself. The world preaches self-glory and inner divinity, but the blood preaches surrender and dependence. It breaks the spirit of self-worship by revealing that all power belongs to God. When you live under the blood, prideful independence turns into humble worship. The blood keeps you grounded in grace, reminding you that true enlightenment is not found in self, but in the Savior. It covers the mind, renews discernment, and guards the heart from deception masked as light.

The blood of Jesus remains the believer's ultimate weapon, unchanging, undefeated, and powerful. Every dark work of the enemy meets its end where the blood is applied.

How to Apply the Blood

Understanding what the Blood does is the first step; learning to apply it is the secret of living in continual victory. In the Old Testament, the Israelites didn't simply believe in the Passover lamb-they applied its blood to their doorposts. Faith in the blood alone would not have saved them; the applied blood did.

So it is with us. The Blood of Jesus has already been shed, but it must be personally received, confessed, and trusted. Revelation 12:11 says, *"They overcame him by the blood of the Lamb and by the word of their testimony."* Your testimony, your spoken agreement with what the Blood has accomplished, activates its power in your life. So, how do you apply the blood?

1. Through Faith.

Romans 3:25 tells us that God presented Jesus *"as a sacrifice of atonement, through faith in His blood."* You apply the Blood first by **believing** that it is enough for you victory. Enough to forgive, cleanse, and restore you completely. Believe that you need nothing more and that in the blood you have all the victory you desire.

2. Through Confession.

The mouth releases what the heart believes. So, when temptation or accusation comes, declare **aloud** what the Blood has done. Say, "I am forgiven through the Blood. I am justified by the Blood. I am healed by the blood. I am protected by the blood. Satan has no claim over me."

3. Through Communion.

Each time we partake of the Lord's Table *(Holy Communion),* we reaffirm that covenant. Jesus said, *"This cup is the new covenant in My blood."* (Luke 22:20). Communion is not ritual, it is remembrance and re-application. As you drink, declare that His Blood still speaks for you.

4. Through Prayer and Worship.

Worship becomes warfare when saturated with the Blood. Begin your prayer times by thanking God for the Blood of Jesus. It brings instant access to His presence and disarms every accusation of the enemy. When you consistently apply the Blood by faith, it becomes your spiritual covering, a shield against condemnation, fear, and the attacks of darkness.

The Blood in Spiritual Warfare

Every attack of the enemy begins with accusation. Satan is called "the accuser of the brethren." (Rev 12:10). He points to your past, magnifies your mistakes, and questions your standing before God. But he is a defeated prosecutor, because the Blood is your eternal evidence of acquittal.

When the enemy whispers, "You don't deserve this victory," answer, "You're right-but Jesus does, and I am in Him." The Blood makes you untouchable because it removes Satan's legal ground. He cannot condemn what God has already cleansed. But if you do not know this, you will continue to beg for victory as if it doesn't belong to you.

In Exodus 12, death could not enter where the blood was applied. In the same way, spiritual death cannot dominate a life covered by Christ's Blood. Plead the Blood over your mind when attacked by anxiety, over your family when fear arises, over your ministry when opposition comes. The Blood still speaks protection and victory.

The Blood and Eternal Victory

The Blood's victory does not end on earth; it extends into eternity because it is an eternal principle. In Revelation 7:14, John saw a multitude clothed in white robes, *"washed... in the blood of the Lamb."* Even in glory, the saints will sing about the Blood. It will forever remind Heaven that grace won, that mercy triumphed, and that love never failed. Satan was cast down because of the Blood; sin lost its sting because of the Blood; death lost its grip because of the Blood. Every victory we will ever experience, now or forever, flows from that same blood.

Let's Recap

Victory through the Blood is the heart of the believer's triumph. The Old Testament revealed the principle: sin demands blood, and covenant requires it. The Passover showed substitution; the cross fulfilled it completely. The Blood of Jesus redeems, justifies, sanctifies, cleanses, protects, gives access, and overcomes. Its power is activated by faith, confession, and continual remembrance.

The Blood silences accusation, heals the conscience, unites the Body, and guarantees eternal life. When you live under the Blood, you live beyond defeat. The accuser may shout, but the Blood speaks louder. It says, "Paid in full." It says, "Righteous." It says, "Beloved." Every time you say "Thank You for the Blood," Heaven echoes, "Victory confirmed."

A Prayer of Thanksgiving for the Blood

Father, thank You for the precious Blood of Jesus-the Lamb without blemish, slain for my redemption. I receive its power over my life today. Let Your Blood cleanse my heart, renew my mind, and silence every accusation of the enemy. I apply the Blood over my family, my home, and my destiny. Because of the Blood, I am forgiven, accepted, protected, and victorious. May I never take it lightly but honor it daily with gratitude and obedience. In Jesus' name, amen.

THE PRINCIPLE OF DIVINE EMPOWERMENT

"Not by might, nor by power, but by My Spirit," says the Lord of hosts. - Zechariah 4:6

In the previous chapter, we saw that victory through the Blood gives us access to forgiveness, redemption, and cleansing. But forgiveness alone does not empower a believer to walk victoriously; it restores the relationship that makes victory possible. The Blood reconciles us to God, yet it is the Holy Spirit who enables us to *live out* that reconciliation. The same Spirit who applies the power of the Blood now equips us to walk daily in triumph.

Without the Holy Spirit, the Christian life becomes impossible. Every attempt to live holy, to love consistently, attain victory or to stand strong against temptation quickly collapses without His presence. The Spirit is not an accessory to the Christian life; He is its essence. He is the continuation of Christ's ministry on earth and the power by which we experience victory in every area.

The Holiness and Majesty of the Holy Spirit

When we think about the Holy Spirit, many imagine warmth, comfort, and peace, and He is indeed all those things. But He is also holy, and His presence demands reverence. In Acts 5:1-10, the story of Ananias and Sapphira reminds us that the Holy Spirit is not to be trifled with. When they lied about their offering, Peter said, *"Ananias, why has Satan filled your heart to lie to the Holy Spirit? You have not lied to men but to God."* (Acts 5:3-4).

This passage reveals the Spirit's divine nature - He is God Himself. The same Spirit who comforts also confronts. The same One who empowers also sanctifies. This account establishes the seriousness of walking with the Holy Spirit: His presence is holy ground. The fear of the Lord is not terror but deep reverence that recognizes His purity and power.

Victory through the Spirit begins with understanding that the One who dwells within us is the same Holy Spirit who struck deceit dead at the altar. When we revere His holiness, we position ourselves for His victory assuring power.

The Necessity of the Spirit

When Jesus told His disciples that He would leave them, sorrow filled their hearts. But He said something profound: *"It is to your advantage that I go away. For if I do not go away, the Helper will not come to you; but if I depart, I will send Him to you."* (John 16:7). Jesus was saying that the indwelling Spirit is better than His physical presence. Through the Spirit, every believer could now experience the same power that once rested upon Christ.

The Holy Spirit is the only power that can translate the victory of Calvary into the reality of daily life. You can know Scripture, attend church, yet still walk in defeat if you ignore the Spirit. The victory of the believer does not come by human willpower or emotional strength; it flows from partnership with the Spirit of God.

He is the breath of victory, the One who brings to life what the Father has promised and what the Son has accomplished. Where the Spirit is ignored, Christianity becomes dry and mechanical. But where He is honored, faith becomes living, prayer becomes power, and obedience becomes joy.

The Person of the Holy Spirit

The Holy Spirit is not an "it"; He is a "He." He is a divine Person with will, emotion, and intellect. He speaks, guides, teaches, and can be grieved. Many see Him merely as a power to be used, but He is *a Person to be known.*

Jesus called Him the Paraklētos, the Helper, Comforter, Advocate, Counselor. The Greek word literally means "one called alongside." He walks beside you to strengthen you, within you to transform you, and before you to lead you. To know the Spirit personally is to live with constant assurance that you are never alone. When fear whispers that you are powerless, the Spirit within whispers back, *"Greater is He who is in you than he who is in the world."* He never abandons, never grows weary, and never fails. Victory begins the moment you stop treating the Holy Spirit as a doctrine and start relating to Him as a daily companion.

In the Old Testament, God's presence dwelled in temples made by hands. Only priests could approach Him, and only under strict conditions. But under the New Covenant, the temple has moved. Paul writes, *"Do you not know that your body is the temple of the*

Holy Spirit who is in you?" (1 Corinthians 6:19).

This truth transforms everything. The glory that once filled Solomon's temple now resides in you. The same power that raised Jesus from the dead now lives within you (Romans 8:11). You are not chasing God's presence; you carry it. Victory is not something you reach for, it's Someone you already host.

The presence of the Spirit turns ordinary people into vessels of extraordinary grace. When you understand that God Himself lives within you, intimidation fades and boldness rises. Every atmosphere you enter is an opportunity for His presence to manifest. Where you go, victory follows, because the Victor lives in you.

There are a few things every believer must understand about the Spirit's role in our lives for them to understand the victory already given to them:

1. The Spirit Convicts and Transforms

Before victory ever shows outwardly, it begins inwardly. The Spirit's first ministry is conviction, not to condemn, but to awaken. Jesus said, *"When He comes, He will convict the world of sin, righteousness, and judgment."* (John 16:8). Conviction is not punishment; it is invitation. The Spirit reveals what must die so that new life can emerge.

When you ignore conviction, you block transformation, when you block transformation, you block victory. But when you yield to conviction, you step into freedom. The Spirit doesn't merely tell you what is wrong; He empowers you to do what is right. He changes appetites, renews thoughts, and heals hidden wounds.

Imagine a believer struggling with anger or bitterness. Each time that emotion rises, the Spirit gently presses on the heart, saying, "Let this go." Yielding in that moment is victory. Every time you choose obedience over offense, peace over pride, you prove that the Spirit is winning the war within.

Transformation is the Spirit's signature miracle. He does not simply improve your behavior; He creates a new nature in you.

2. The Spirit Teaches and Reveals

Jesus called the Spirit *"the Spirit of truth."* (John 16:13). He is the one who makes the Word come alive. Without Him, Scripture remains information; with Him, it becomes revelation. He turns logos into rhema, written truth into living voice.

When you read the Bible with the Holy Spirit, verses you've seen a hundred times suddenly explode with meaning. He connects the Word to your present situation, showing you how to walk in victory. Think of Peter before Pentecost, confused, fearful, inconsistent. Yet after the Spirit came upon him, the same Peter stood boldly before thousands, preaching with clarity and power. What changed? The Spirit turned knowledge into revelation, and revelation into boldness.

In your own life, the Spirit still teaches this way. He reminds you of promises when you're weary, exposes lies when you're deceived, and shows you the path of wisdom when you're uncertain. Every victory begins with revelation.

3. The Spirit Guides

Romans 8:14 says, *"For all who are led by the Spirit of God are sons of God."* To be led is not to be driven. The devil drives by pressure; the Spirit leads by peace. He guides step by step, often through gentle impressions, inner witness, or quiet conviction.

The guidance of the Spirit is one of the greatest proofs of God's love. He doesn't just save you and leave you to figure life out, He walks you through it. He knows the traps the enemy has set, the relationships that will bless or break you, and the timing of every breakthrough.

Learning to follow His leading is the key to consistent victory. Many defeats happen not because we are weak, but because we moved ahead of the Spirit. Waiting on Him may feel slow, but it saves you from years of regret. When you sense His prompt to pause, pause. When He nudges you to speak, speak. Every act of obedience enlarges your capacity for victory.

Learning to Hear the Spirit's Voice

The Spirit speaks in many ways. To walk in victory, we must know His voice and recognize how He communicates. Here are seven primary ways the Holy Spirit speaks to His people:

Through His Word (2 Timothy 3:16; 2 Peter 1:20-21): The Spirit's first language is Scripture. Every sentence in the Bible was breathed out by Him, and He never contradicts what He has already written. A believer who stays rooted in the Word will not be easily misled, because the Spirit always speaks in harmony with His book. Often, when you read a passage you have read many times before, a single verse seems to rise from the page with new power-that is the Spirit's voice. In moments of confusion, He draws a line of truth through Scripture that steadies your heart. The more you know the Word, the more familiar you become with the sound of His guidance.

Through the Inner Witness (Acts 8:29): Sometimes the Spirit speaks not through audible words but through inward peace. He gives a gentle but firm assurance that says, "This is the way." Philip experienced this when the Spirit prompted him, "Go and join that chariot." It wasn't thunder; it was an inward nudge. In daily life, you may sense a quiet conviction to speak to someone, to pause before making a decision, or to move in a new direction. That is the inner witness. It is never frantic or fearful; it is steady and sure. Learning to trust that witness is key to walking in victory because it keeps you in step with His timing.

Through the Gathered Church (1 Corinthians 14:29): The Spirit speaks through community. He uses pastors, teachers, and fellow believers to confirm direction and sharpen discernment. In Acts 13, the prophets and teachers at Antioch were worshiping when the Spirit said, *"Set apart Barnabas and Saul."* The instruction came through a collective hearing. In the same way, God often uses a sermon, a word of encouragement, or even casual fellowship to confirm what He has already placed in your heart. The Spirit loves unity, and His voice often grows clearer when you are surrounded by Spirit-filled counsel rather than isolated opinion.

Through the Gifts of God (1 Corinthians 12): The Holy Spirit distributes gifts-prophecy, wisdom, knowledge, discernment, healing-as tools for building faith and revealing divine insight. These gifts are not for show; they are for service. When a prophetic word exposes something hidden or brings direction that aligns with Scripture, the Spirit is speaking. Imagine a time in prayer when a believer shares a simple word of knowledge about someone's hidden struggle, and it unlocks repentance and healing. That is how the Spirit uses gifts-to reveal Jesus, not to elevate people. Every genuine manifestation of the gifts will glorify Christ and edify His church. I have a seven part series on "The Gifts of God" on the Verse Connect YouTube Channel to help you understand how all these gifts work.

Through Circumstances (1 Corinthians 16:8-9): The Spirit opens and closes doors to guide you into purpose. Paul recognized this when he wrote, *"A great and effective door has opened to me."* Sometimes resistance itself becomes guidance, when one path consistently blocks and another unfolds smoothly, the Spirit may be redirecting you. He orchestrates divine appointments and coincidences that are too precise to be random. A conversation with a stranger, an unexpected delay, or a sudden opportunity can all be His way of steering your steps. The Spirit governs circumstances to ensure you are always positioned for victory, even when you don't yet see the pattern.

Through Dreams and Visions (Joel 2:28): The Spirit often speaks in pictures. Dreams and visions are His way of revealing what natural eyes cannot see. In Scripture, Joseph, Daniel, and Peter all received guidance through the night. A dream may highlight an area of warning or affirm a promise; a vision may open your eyes to pray strategically. These impressions will always agree with Scripture and draw you closer to Christ. When the Spirit paints images on your heart, write them down, pray over them, and seek confirmation through the Word. They are glimpses of God's intention, designed to bring direction, not confusion.

Through Prayer and Communion (Romans 8:26-27): Prayer is the atmosphere where the Spirit's voice is clearest. In those moments of stillness before God, He brings Scriptures to remembrance, stirs holy desires, and intercedes through groanings too deep for words. Many believers testify that while praying for one need, the Spirit redirected them toward another, revealing God's true agenda. Communion with the Spirit transforms prayer from monologue to conversation. The more time you spend in His presence, the more His thoughts blend with yours. In that sacred exchange, burdens lift, clarity comes, and you find yourself walking in step with the will of the Father.

These are not seven separate voices but seven expressions of one faithful Voice, the Spirit of Truth. The Holy Spirit's voice is gentle, calm, and life-giving; the flesh's voice is impulsive, fearful, and self-centered.

The voice of the Holy Spirit is gentle, reassuring, and patient, while the voice of the flesh is harsh, anxious, and rushed. The Spirit's words always build faith and exalt Christ, but the flesh promotes self, fear, and pride. The Spirit leads toward holiness and peace, while the flesh drives toward compromise and confusion. When you follow the Spirit's voice, the result is life, freedom, and clarity; when you follow the flesh, it produces guilt, frustration, and bondage.

The Holy Spirit remains steady and unchanging, but the voice of the flesh shifts with moods, emotions, and circumstances. When you are unsure, measure every impression by these fruits. The Spirit never contradicts the Word or the nature of Jesus.

Victory through D.I.S.C.E.R.N (Discernment)

Victory is not just avoiding sin; it's avoiding deception. The Spirit is the believer's radar in a world full of counterfeits. Jesus said, *"When He, the Spirit of truth, comes, He will guide you into all truth."*

(John 16:13).

Discernment is not suspicion; it is spiritual clarity. The Holy Spirit reveals motives, warns of traps, and gives wisdom for decisions. Many defeats in life come not from disobedience but from ignorance, stepping into things that look good but aren't God. The Spirit sees ahead; He knows the unseen.

Imagine being offered a business deal that seems perfect. Everyone says, "This is it." But as you pray, something feels unsettled. That unrest is the Spirit guarding you. Later, you discover the deal was fraudulent. What looked like caution was actually deliverance. That's victory, won in silence before the battle ever began. Walking in the Spirit means letting peace be your compass. If there is no peace, pause. The Spirit's leading will never contradict His Word or rob your peace.

The Holy Spirit is constantly speaking, guiding, and revealing God's will, but so many voices compete for our attention. The voice of the world, the voice of our flesh, and the voice of the enemy. How then do we know which voice is truly God's? The answer is found in the discipline of discernment. God never leaves His people confused; He provides a framework to test every word and impression. The acronym D.I.S.C.E.R.N. will help you weigh what you hear so that you can walk confidently in truth and victory.

D - Doctrine

The first test of any voice or revelation is Doctrine. Does it align with Scripture? God never contradicts His Word, and the Holy Spirit never leads where the Word forbids. "Heaven and earth will pass away, but My words will never pass away." (Matthew 24:35). Doctrine is the foundation of discernment, if it disagrees with the

Bible, it cannot be the Holy Spirit.

For example, if you ever sense a voice telling you, "It's okay, everyone sins, just do it and repent later," stop immediately. That voice is not from God, it violates Romans 6:1, "*Shall we continue in sin that grace may abound? Certainly not!*" The Spirit convicts, He never condones. Doctrine protects you from deception by anchoring your hearing in the written Word. When the Word is your filter, lies lose their power.

I - Inner Witness

The second test is the Inner Witness. The Holy Spirit communicates peace that surpasses understanding. When something is truly from Him, there's a steady calm, even if the instruction challenges your comfort zone. Colossians 3:15 says, "*Let the peace of Christ rule in your hearts.*" That word rule means to act as an umpire, making the call between right and wrong.

Sometimes, the Spirit's witness is a gentle unease, a check that something isn't right. Perhaps you were about to enter a partnership or make a purchase, and suddenly peace disappears. That's the Spirit's warning. I remember a believer who was offered a dream job overseas.

Everything looked perfect, but she couldn't shake the unrest in her spirit. Months later, that company collapsed in scandal. The Spirit had protected her by removing peace. When peace lifts, pause. When peace remains, proceed.

S - Support

The third test is Support. God confirms His direction through the counsel of mature, Spirit-filled believers. Proverbs 11:14 says, *"In the multitude of counselors there is safety."* The same Spirit who speaks to you also speaks through others in the Body of Christ. True revelation stands strong when tested in community.

Suppose you believe the Lord has called you to a new ministry or major decision. Before running ahead, share it with trusted spiritual mentors who know God's voice. If every mature believer who loves you and walks closely with the Lord hesitates, slow down. The Spirit never leads you into isolation or pride. He weaves unity through confirmation. When godly voices echo what you've heard privately, that's support from Heaven saying, "Move forward."

C - Character

The fourth test is Character. Jesus said, *"By their fruits you will know them."* (Matthew 7:16). The Holy Spirit always produces fruit that looks like Christ, love, joy, peace, patience, kindness, goodness, faithfulness, gentleness, and self-control (Galatians 5:22–23). Any word, teaching, or prophecy that breeds pride, anger, division, or greed does not come from the Spirit of God.

Consider a preacher or influencer who claims to carry a revelation from God but whose life is filled with manipulation, arrogance, or immorality. The Spirit may use anyone, but He does not dwell in hypocrisy. The fruit reveals the root. Likewise, when you sense a prompting that leads you to act in love, humility, or forgiveness, you can trust that it's the Spirit's voice. The Holy Spirit's words always shape your character before they shift your circumstances.

E - Exaltation

The fifth test is Exaltation. The Holy Spirit always glorifies Jesus. He never points to human ego, personal agenda, or selfish ambition. Jesus said in John 16:14, *"He will glorify Me, for He will take what is Mine and declare it to you."* Every true work of the Spirit magnifies Christ and draws hearts to Him.

If a message or manifestation leaves you impressed with a person instead of worshiping Jesus, something is wrong. For example, a genuine healing service leaves people saying, "Look what Jesus has done!" not, "Look how powerful that preacher is!" The Spirit exalts the Savior, not the servant. If the spotlight shifts from Christ to charisma, that's not the Holy Spirit. Victory comes when you follow the voice that keeps your eyes fixed on Jesus, not on personalities.

R - Reliability

The sixth test is Reliability. God's character is consistent; He is not capricious or unstable. The same Spirit who spoke yesterday will not contradict Himself today. *"Jesus Christ is the same yesterday, today, and forever."* (Hebrews 13:8). The Spirit's voice always harmonizes with His nature, holy, loving, and faithful.

Imagine someone who says, "God told me to do this," but a few days later says, "God changed His mind." God is not confused. While He may unfold details progressively, His moral will never shifts. Reliability means that the voice you follow leads to stability, not chaos. When you look back, the Spirit's leading will always make sense in the light of His Word and character. He is trustworthy, predictable in His goodness, and unwavering in His truth.

123

N - Narrative

Finally, the test of Narrative. Every voice builds a storyline. The Holy Spirit's narrative always leads toward holiness, surrender, and Christlikeness. The enemy's narrative leads toward self-promotion, greed, and compromise. You must ask, "Where is this leading me in six months or six years?" The Spirit's story for your life is always redemptive.

Picture a believer who hears an invitation to start a business. If the idea draws them closer to God, increases generosity, and creates opportunities to serve others, the narrative is holy. But if that same idea breeds pride, dishonesty, and spiritual drift, the narrative has shifted, and so has the source. The Spirit's direction will never steer you away from the cross or away from the fruit of righteousness. His storyline always ends with glory to God and victory for His people.

When you live by these seven filters: Doctrine, Inner Witness, Support, Character, Exaltation, Reliability, and Narrative, you remove confusion and protect your destiny. Discernment is not suspicion; it is Spirit-led clarity. Every believer can learn to discern because every believer carries the Spirit of Truth. The more you exercise these principles, the sharper your hearing becomes, and the more consistent your victories become.

The enemy thrives on confusion, but the Spirit leads in peace. When you learn to D.I.S.C.E.R.N., you will no longer stumble through life hoping for direction, you will walk with confidence, knowing that Heaven is guiding your every step. When you apply this framework, you eliminate confusion. Victory is impossible without discernment, and discernment is impossible without the Spirit.

"If we live by the Spirit, let us also walk by the Spirit." - Galatians 5:25

The first part of this chapter revealed who the Holy Spirit is and what His presence means for every believer. But knowing who He is must now become walking with Him daily. Victory through the Holy Spirit is not only about awareness, it is about alignment. The Spirit-filled life is a partnership: you yield, He empowers. You obey, He manifests. You trust, He triumphs through you.

Many believers love the Holy Spirit's presence in church but ignore His leadership in life. They sing "Holy Spirit, You are welcome here," but then make decisions without Him, speak words He never inspired, and live under pressures He could have guided them around. The Spirit does not just visit revival meetings; He leads everyday life. Victory flows not from a single encounter but from continual fellowship.

The Spirit Produces the Fruit of Victory

True victory is not measured by external success but by internal fruit. The evidence of the Spirit's rule is not in the noise of gifts but in the quietness of character. *"The fruit of the Spirit is love, joy, peace, patience, kindness, goodness, faithfulness, gentleness, and self-control."* (Galatians 5:22–23).

Fruit is proof of partnership. The more you walk with Him, the more you look like Him. The fruit of the Spirit is the culture of Heaven reproduced in human hearts. Love overcomes hatred; peace overcomes fear; joy overcomes sorrow.

Imagine a believer facing constant criticism at work. The flesh wants to retaliate, but the Spirit births patience. As they respond with gentleness, the atmosphere begins to change. Others take notice, not because they preached a sermon but because they lived one. That's what the fruit of the Spirit does: it silently wins battles that words cannot.

Victory through the Holy Spirit is not dramatic; it is transformational. When your reactions start resembling Jesus, you are already walking in triumph.

The Spirit Empowers Boldness

Acts 4:31 says, *"They were all filled with the Holy Spirit, and they spoke the Word of God with boldness."* Fear paralyzes; the Spirit mobilizes. Where fear locks doors, the Spirit opens mouths.

The disciples hid after Jesus' crucifixion, but after Pentecost, those same men confronted rulers, endured persecution, and rejoiced that they were counted worthy to suffer for His name. What changed? The Spirit replaced fear with fire.

You cannot live victoriously while bound by fear. Whether it's fear of rejection, failure, or sickness, the Holy Spirit emboldens the believer to stand in faith. He whispers, "You are not alone," and suddenly courage rises where anxiety once reigned.

Boldness does not mean arrogance; it means confidence in divine backing. When the Spirit fills you, you stop calculating risks and start trusting results. You move when He says move, speak when He says speak, and rest when He says rest. Every act of obedience releases victory.

Let's Recap

Victory through the Holy Spirit is not about striving, it's about surrender. He is not a distant force but the very presence of God within you, teaching, guiding, empowering, and comforting you. Through Him, you receive wisdom for every decision, strength for every weakness, and peace for every storm.

When you yield to His leading, fear loses its grip, confusion fades, and your life begins to mirror the power of Jesus. The Spirit doesn't just visit you-He lives in you, walks with you, and works through you. Victory is no longer a moment; it becomes a lifestyle of partnership with Him.

The same Spirit who raised Christ from the dead lives in you. That means defeat can never be your final story. Walking in step with Him is walking in continual triumph.

A Prayer for the Holy Spirit's Power

Holy Spirit, thank You for being my Helper, my Comforter, and my power for living. I surrender my heart and every part of my life to You. Lead me, teach me, and fill me afresh today. Help me to hear Your voice clearly and to obey quickly. Let Your fruit grow in me and Your gifts flow through me.

Where I have been weak, be my strength. Where I have been afraid, be my courage. Let Your presence go before me and Your power rest upon me. I choose to walk in step with You, to live in victory, and to glorify Jesus in all that I do. Amen.

CHAPTER

8

THE PRINCIPLE OF ALIGNMENT

"The prayer of a righteous man is powerful and effective." - James 5:16

Victory requires alignment with God's perfect will. A believer aligns through prayer. Prayer is the breath of the spirit and the heartbeat of the believer's walk with God. A Christian without prayer is like a soldier without communication on the battlefield - vulnerable, isolated, and easily defeated. Prayer is not just a discipline; it is a lifeline. It's a matter of life and death. Through it, Heaven touches earth and man communes with God.

From Genesis to Revelation, victory has always been birthed in the place of prayer. Before God moves on earth, He first moves in the hearts of those who pray. Elijah prayed, and fire fell. Hannah prayed, and a barren womb became fruitful. Daniel prayed, and kings' decrees were overturned. Jesus prayed, and the world was redeemed.

Prayer is not convincing God to do something He is reluctant to do; it is aligning ourselves with what He is already willing to do. It is not twisting His arm - it is taking hold of His heart.

The Design of Prayer - Created for Communion

Prayer did not begin as a religious act; it began as relationship and it must stay that way. In Eden, before sin entered, Adam and God spoke daily. There was no ritual, no request list - only communion. Adam didn't pray to get things from God; he prayed because he had God. When sin broke that fellowship, prayer became the bridge back to intimacy. That is why Jesus often withdrew to lonely places to pray (Luke 5:16). He was not escaping the world; He was aligning with the Father. Prayer was His secret place of strength.

If Jesus - the Son of God - needed prayer to fulfill His purpose, how much more do we? Prayer is the oxygen of spiritual life. Without it, faith suffocates, discernment dims, and peace fades.

The Priority of Prayer

The first church was birthed in a prayer meeting (Acts 2). The early believers did not begin by planning structures or strategies - they began by waiting, praying, and listening. From that upper room, the world was changed.

Today, we often reverse that order: we plan, strategize, and then pray as an afterthought. But true victory begins when prayer is not a supplement to our plans but the foundation of them. Jesus said, *"My house shall be called a house of prayer."* (Matthew 21:13). This means the atmosphere of God's presence is sustained through prayer. When prayer ceases, power fades. When prayer flows, power grows.

Prayer does not just change things; it changes us. It burns pride, refines motives, and teaches patience. It moves us from anxiety to trust, from striving to surrender.

Prayer as Relationship, Not Routine

Many people struggle with prayer because they see it as a performance rather than a relationship. They think effective prayer requires special words, tones, or postures. But God is not impressed by eloquence; He responds to sincerity.

Jesus warned against "vain repetitions," reminding us that the Father already knows what we need before we ask (Matthew 6:7-8). Prayer is not informing God - it is inviting Him. It is fellowship, not formality.

Think of a child speaking to a loving parent. The value of that conversation is not in perfect grammar but in genuine connection. Likewise, God delights not in polished speech but in honest hearts. Prayer becomes powerful when it becomes personal. When you stop praying to sound spiritual and start praying to know God, Heaven opens.

The Example of Jesus in Prayer

No life demonstrated victory through prayer more than Jesus'. Though He was God in the flesh, He lived in constant dependence on the Father through prayer.

He prayed at dawn (Mark 1:35), before miracles (John 11:41-42), before choosing disciples (Luke 6:12), before the cross (Luke 22:42), and even on the cross ("Father, forgive them"). His strength flowed from His secret place. The disciples noticed this and never asked Him, "Teach us to preach," or "Teach us to perform miracles." They said, *"Lord, teach us to pray."* (Luke 11:1). They realized that everything Jesus did publicly was sustained by what He did privately.

The Lord's Prayer was His answer - a model of priorities: worship first *("Hallowed be Your Name"),* surrender (*"Your kingdom come"*), dependence (*"Give us daily bread"*), repentance, and intercession. True prayer aligns earth with Heaven. Jesus prayed not to impress God but to stay in union with Him. And that is where our victory begins - when prayer becomes our connection, not our ceremony.

The Heart That Heaven Hears

For prayer to produce victory, it must come from a surrendered heart. God is not moved by volume but by humility. 2 Chronicles 7:14 says, *"If My people who are called by My Name will humble themselves and pray, and seek My face..."* Notice - humility comes before prayer. Pride prays to be seen; humility prays to be changed.

David said, *"The Lord is near to the brokenhearted."* (Psalm 34:18). The prayer that reaches Heaven often starts with a heart broken before God. Effective prayer also requires faith. Hebrews 11:6 says, "Without faith it is impossible to please God." Faith is the assurance that God not only hears but will answer according to His wisdom and timing. Prayer without faith is just talk; prayer with faith is transformation. When faith and humility meet, Heaven responds.

"The weapons of our warfare are not carnal, but mighty through God for the pulling down of strongholds." - 2 Corinthians 10:4

Prayer is not just communion; it is combat. It is both intimacy and warfare. In prayer, we exchange weakness for strength, fear for faith, and uncertainty for divine instruction. Prayer is the believer's spiritual artillery - unseen, yet unstoppable.

When you pray, you engage Heaven's power against hell's resistance. Prayer moves the invisible world and influences the visible one. That is why Satan fears praying believers more than preaching believers - because prayer enforces what preaching declares.

Daniel understood this. For twenty-one days he prayed and fasted, and though the answer was dispatched from Heaven on the first day, a demonic prince resisted it (Daniel 10:12–13). Daniel didn't quit - he persisted until breakthrough came.

Prayer is how we stand in spiritual authority. Ephesians 6 describes the armor of God and concludes, *"Praying always with all prayer and supplication in the Spirit."* (Ephesians 6:18). Prayer activates the armor and sustains the battle. When believers pray, angels are mobilized, demonic plots are dismantled, and divine purposes are fulfilled. Prayer doesn't make God move reluctantly; it positions us to partner with His movement.

How to Pray Effectively

   1. **Pray the Word.**

God's Word is His will. 1 John 5:14 says, *"If we ask anything according to His will, He hears us."* The most effective prayers are Word-based. When you quote Scripture in prayer, you remind Heaven of what God has already promised and silence the lies of the enemy.

   2. **Pray in the Spirit.**

The Holy Spirit energizes and directs prayer. Romans 8:26 says,

"The Spirit Himself intercedes for us." Praying in tongues or Spirit-led prayer releases mysteries beyond human understanding and aligns your heart with God's perfect plan.

3. Pray with Faith.

Faith transforms requests into declarations. Jesus said, *"Whatever you ask for in prayer, believe that you have received it, and it will be yours."* (Mark 11:24). Faith sees results before they appear.

4. Pray with Persistence.

Jesus taught, *"Men ought always to pray and not to faint."* (Luke 18:1). Persistence does not convince God; it conquers doubt. Keep praying until peace replaces pressure - that's when victory is sealed.

5. Pray with Thanksgiving.

Philippians 4:6 teaches us to present requests *"with thanksgiving."* Gratitude shifts the atmosphere from worry to worship. Thankfulness invites God's presence and keeps your heart anchored in trust.

The Power of Agreement

There is multiplied power in united prayer. Jesus said, *"If two of you agree on earth about anything they ask, it will be done for them by My Father in heaven."* (Matthew 18:19).

When believers join in one accord, Heaven leans in. That's why Satan works so hard to divide families and churches - because he knows a united church is an unstoppable church. In Acts 4, after Peter and John were threatened, the believers gathered and *"lifted their voices together to God."* The result? *"The place where they were meeting was shaken."* (Acts 4:31). When hearts agree, power increases.

Obstacles to Effective Prayer

Every believer faces resistance in prayer. Sometimes the obstacle is external; other times it's internal. *Unforgiveness* - Mark 11:25 warns that bitterness blocks prayer. Forgiveness unclogs the spiritual pipeline of grace. *Doubt* - James 1:6 says the one who doubts *"is like a wave of the sea, blown and tossed by the wind."* Faith anchors prayer. *Disobedience* - 1 John 3:22 reminds us that we receive what we ask because "we keep His commandments." Obedience sustains authority. *Distraction* - Noise dulls discernment. That's why Jesus often withdrew to quiet places. Prayer thrives in focus. *Pride* – Makes you think you can do it on your own.

When you identify and remove these hindrances, prayer becomes not a struggle but a flow.

Prayer and the Presence

The true reward of prayer is not answers but presence. Answers are gifts; presence is relationship. Moses understood this when he said, *"If Your presence does not go with us, do not send us up from here."* (Exodus 33:15).

In prayer, we don't just seek God's hand - we seek His face. When you spend time with Him, His peace begins to fill every anxious place. The longer you stay, the more His presence redefines your priorities. Many begin prayer seeking solutions and end it transformed. The situation might still look the same, but the heart is no longer fearful. That is victory - when peace replaces panic.

Living a Lifestyle of Prayer

Paul wrote, *"Pray without ceasing."* (1 Thessalonians 5:17). This doesn't mean spending every moment on your knees; it means maintaining constant communion. You can pray while driving, working, or walking - because prayer is not location-based; it is connection-based.

When prayer becomes lifestyle, you live in continual awareness of God's presence. You begin each day saying, "Good morning, Holy Spirit," and end each night saying, "Thank You, Father." This keeps your heart tender and your spirit alert. Your actions after "amen" are the continuation of your payer. Most of us have prayed heartfelt prayers and went on to cancel everything we prayed about through our opposite actions.

A lifestyle of prayer protects you from spiritual dryness. It keeps the fire burning when circumstances try to dim it. The devil's first target is always your prayer life, because once prayer stops, power fades. Guard it like treasure.

Let's Recap

Victory through prayer means walking in partnership and power with God through constant communion. Prayer is relationship first and warfare second. It aligns our hearts with God's will and releases His power on earth. Jesus modeled a life of prayer that produced constant victory.

Effective prayer is rooted in humility, faith, and obedience. Prayer is our greatest weapon against spiritual opposition. The Word, the Spirit, and persistence make prayer unstoppable. The goal of prayer is not just answers but the presence of God Himself. When prayer becomes your habit, victory becomes your rhythm.

A Prayer for a Victorious Prayer Life

Father, thank You for the privilege of prayer - the gateway to Your heart and the weapon of my victory. Teach me to pray not just when I need something, but because I love Your presence. Fill me with faith when I pray and patience while I wait. Remove distractions and strengthen my spirit. Let my words align with Your will, and let Your peace guard my heart. Through prayer, may I live in constant victory, resting in Your power and rejoicing in Your presence. In Jesus' Name, amen.

Part Two

VICTORY IN THE SOUL

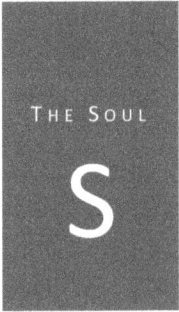

REPOSITIONING OF THE MIND

"Do not be conformed to this world, but be transformed by the renewing of your mind, that you may prove what is that good and acceptable and perfect will of God." - Romans 12:2

Now that you know all these principles for victory, it is important to understand the part of you that often wrestles against them - the soul. The soul is the meeting place of your thoughts, emotions, desires, and will. It is the part of you that feels, remembers, processes, reacts, and chooses.

While your spirit was made alive in Christ the moment you were saved, your soul is still being shaped, renewed, and transformed into the image of Jesus. This is why some days you feel victorious and other days you feel overwhelmed. Your spirit already agrees with God, but your soul is learning to. The battle you often sense is not a contradiction of your salvation - it is the collision between an awakened spirit and an unrenewed soul.

The soul is not your enemy; it is your responsibility. David spoke to his soul, commanded his soul, even questioned his soul. *"Why are you cast down, O my soul?"* he asked. The psalmist understood what many believers ignore: your soul must be shepherded. If left unattended, the soul gravitates toward fear, comparison, anxiety, impatience, and self-preservation.

But when surrendered to the Holy Spirit and anchored in truth, the soul becomes a powerful instrument of obedience and worship. Scripture calls the soul the seat of your decision-making, the place where you choose whether you will believe God or bow to circumstance. This is why transformation does not begin in your environment but within the soul.

Understand this: the soul was never meant to lead; it was meant to follow. When the soul leads, life becomes unstable - tossed by emotion, swayed by pressure, and governed by circumstances. But when the soul follows the spirit, strength rises, clarity returns, and peace becomes natural. The renewed soul aligns with God's Word, resists the enemy's whispers, and agrees with Heaven's agenda. This is what Paul meant when he wrote, *"Be transformed by the renewing of your mind."* He was speaking about the soul - about the process of bringing your inner world into agreement with the truths God has already spoken.

Victory becomes real the moment your soul bows to truth. The moment your feelings submit to faith. The moment your desires align with God's will. The moment your will chooses the instruction rather than the impulse. Your spirit already knows the path of victory, but your soul must learn to walk in it. That is the journey of every believer - not trying to become victorious, but training the soul to believe what the spirit already knows: that through Christ, you are more than a conqueror.

If you do not disciple your soul, life will. And life is a cruel teacher.

But the Holy Spirit is gentle, patient, and relentless. He whispers to your soul when you feel overwhelmed. He steadies your soul when disappointment shakes you. He corrects your soul when pride rises. He restores your soul when pain exhausts you. Every principle in this book rests on this truth: your soul must come under the leadership of the Spirit if you are going to walk in sustained victory.

So as you move forward, remember this - your spirit is saved instantly, but your soul is saved gradually. And that process is not proof of weakness; it is proof of God's ongoing work in you. Let the Word renew your mind. Let worship stabilize your emotions. Let prayer soften your will. Let obedience train your desires. Let surrender unclutter your inner world. When your soul begins to echo what Heaven has already declared, victory ceases to be a concept and becomes your reality.

Your soul is not a battlefield to fear - it is a territory God intends to conquer with truth. And as truth takes ground within you, every part of your life will rise to match it. Paul, in the book of Romans, spends the first eleven chapters establishing the gospel, teaching about sin, justification, and the grace of God. But when we get to Romans 12, there is a shift. Paul moves from what Christ has done to how we now live because of it. The first two verses of Romans 12 serve as a divine blueprint for victorious living.

He begins by addressing three parts of human existence: the body, the soul, and the spirit. *"Present your bodies as a living sacrifice, holy and acceptable to God"*, this speaks to the body. *"Be transformed by the renewing of your mind"*, this speaks to the soul. And *"by faith we live"*, this speaks to the spirit. The victory of the believer lies in the alignment of these three, when the body, soul, and spirit work in harmony under the leadership of the Holy Spirit.

The Inner Conflict

Jesus said, *"The spirit is willing, but the flesh is weak."* (Matthew 26:41). Paul echoed this in Romans 7:15–20 when he confessed, *"What I want to do I do not do, but what I hate I do."* These verses reveal an age-old struggle, the battle between the spirit and the flesh, between what God desires and what our human nature wants.

Every believer experiences this tension. The spirit longs for holiness, but the body craves comfort. The spirit desires prayer, but the flesh prefers sleep. The spirit wants forgiveness, but the mind rehearses offenses. Victory comes when the mind, the bridge between body and spirit, is transformed to side with the Spirit of God. The renewed mind becomes the deciding vote between flesh and spirit.

When your mind is renewed, your body follows the spirit instead of fighting it. The victory you've been praying for doesn't start in your circumstances; it starts in your thoughts. What fills your mind will eventually shape your life. *"As a man thinketh, so is he."*

Why the Mind Matters

The mind is not merely your brain; it is the seat of thought, emotion, belief, and consciousness. It interprets both spiritual and physical. The enemy understands this, which is why every attack begins with a thought. Fear begins as a thought. Temptation begins as a thought. Doubt begins as a thought. The mind is the battlefield of destiny.

A transformed mind is a protected mind. The world trains people to think in patterns of fear, pride, greed, and self-sufficiency. But God calls His children to think with faith, humility, generosity, and surrender. Until your mind is renewed, your spirit can be filled with truth while your life still reflects bondage.

The key to victory, then, is not trying harder but thinking higher. Transformation begins when the Word of God replaces the patterns of the world in your mind.

1. Thinking, The First Proof of a Renewed Mind

Everyone thinks, but not everyone thinks correctly. There is a prescribed heavenly thought process we must unconditionally subscribe to. A transformed mind begins with transformed thinking. Philippians 4:8 instructs, *"Whatever is true, whatever is noble, whatever is right, whatever is pure, whatever is lovely, whatever is admirable, if anything is excellent or praiseworthy, think about such things."*

The way you think determines how you live. If your thoughts are filled with defeat, fear, and limitation, your life will reflect those patterns. But when your thoughts are filled with faith, gratitude, and God's promises, your life begins to mirror heaven's reality.

Imagine a person facing a medical diagnosis. The world teaches them to fear, to expect the worst, to prepare for loss. But a renewed mind says, *"By His stripes, I am healed."* It's not denial, it's declaration. It's choosing to think according to God's truth rather than worldly probability. Victory through the mind starts with refusing to let fear have the final word.

2. Rejecting Worldly Patterns

Romans 12:2 doesn't just say *"be transformed"*; it also says, *"Do not conform."* Transformation is not possible if you're still fitting into the world's mold. Worldly patterns teach self-promotion, comparison, and instant gratification. God's kingdom teaches humility, contentment, and process.

A believer with a renewed mind questions the source of their thoughts: Why do I think this way? Where did this belief come from? Does it agree with Scripture?

For example, society glorifies wealth and status, even if that comes without purpose. But the mind of Christ sees wealth as a tool for generosity. The world teaches revenge as strength; the Spirit teaches forgiveness as victory. Every time you reject the world's mindset and embrace God's truth, you win another round in the battle for your mind.

3. Speech - The Voice of a Renewed Mind

Speech reveals the state of the heart. Jesus said, *"Out of the abundance of the heart, the mouth speaks."* (Luke 6:45). Words are not harmless, they are creative. You were not designed to speak anything you were not willing to create in your life. Every word you release shapes your environment.

A renewed mind refuses to say what it does not want to see. You cannot expect a victorious life while your mouth agrees with defeat. Whatever you declare with your mouth, the spiritual realm has no choice but to agree, it is a principle. The victorious understand that the language of faith is the language of victory.

Think of a believer who constantly says, "Nothing ever works out for me." Their words are seeds of defeat. But another believer, facing the same challenge, declares, "All things work together for my good." One sees obstacles, the other sees opportunity. Both are right, because both will live the fruit of their words.

4. Becoming - The Process of Transformation

Transformation is not instant; it's progressive. *"We all, with unveiled faces, beholding as in a mirror the glory of the Lord, are being transformed into the same image from glory to glory."* (2 Corinthians 3:18). A renewed mind embraces process. It understands that God changes us in stages. The world says, "Fix yourself." The Spirit says, "Surrender yourself." Transformation is not self-improvement; it is Spirit-empowered surrender.

Becoming is not about trying harder but yielding deeper. You are not responsible for the transformation, only for the surrender. The Holy Spirit does the transforming. Victory through the mind comes when you stop striving and start yielding. It is counter intuitive I know, but this is the most potent strategy of victory.

5. The Word - The Tool for Renewal

The Word of God is the only instrument that can truly renew the mind. Hebrews 4:12 declares, *"For the Word of God is living and active... sharper than any two-edged sword."*

You do not renew your mind through motivational speeches or earthly meditation. You renew it by immersing yourself in Scripture. The Word of God is not information; it's transformation. Every time you read it, your thinking adjusts to heaven's frequency.

A believer battling addiction, for example, doesn't just need willpower, they need Word power. When Scripture fills your thoughts, it uproots lies and plants truth. The Word trains the mind to agree with what God has already declared about you.

6. Community - The Company That Shapes the Mind

Transformation doesn't happen in isolation. Proverbs 13:20 says, *"He who walks with the wise becomes wise."* The people around you either reinforce your old thinking or encourage your new mindset.

If you want victory in your thought life, surround yourself with people who speak faith, not fear. Be around believers who remind you of your identity, not your failures. Community is God's safety net for the renewing mind.

Even Jesus walked with disciples, not crowds. A renewed mind chooses fellowship that feeds the spirit, not gossip that fuels the flesh. The right environment accelerates renewal; the wrong one destroys it.

The Spirit's Role in Transformation

Romans 8:5 says, *"Those who live according to the Spirit have their minds set on what the Spirit desires."* The Holy Spirit is the one who changes the inner narrative. Without Him, every attempt at renewal becomes human effort.

When you invite the Spirit to lead your thinking, He convicts, corrects, and comforts. He helps you take thoughts captive and teaches you to replace lies with truth. As you learned in the previous chapter, He doesn't just give power, He gives perspective. Victory through the mind is impossible without the Spirit. He is the one who renews, reforms, and realigns. Transformation is His specialty; surrender is yours.

Renewed Thinking and Victory in Daily Life

A renewed mind affects every area, faith, health, relationships, and purpose. The renewed mind turns obstacles into opportunities.

A believer who has lost a job doesn't spiral into despair; they declare, "God is opening a new door." A student facing failure doesn't quit; they see it as training ground for growth. A person battling anxiety doesn't give in to fear; they renew their mind with "Be anxious for nothing." When your mind is transformed, your perception changes. And when perception changes, your reality follows.

Victory begins in the mind. It's the place where heaven's truth meets human thought. When your mind agrees with God's Word, your life aligns with His will. The mind is the soil of transformation; what you plant there will grow in your life.

Romans 12:2 isn't a suggestion; it's a heavenly strategy for victory. You can't walk in God's perfect will with a worldly mindset. Let the Word shape your thoughts, the Spirit guide your perspective, and your surrender open the door for transformation. The renewed mind doesn't just survive, it reigns.

"When he came to himself, he said, 'How many of my father's hired servants have bread enough to spare, and I perish with hunger!'" - Luke 15:17

The story of the prodigal son is more than a parable of forgiveness; it's a blueprint for mind renewal. It reveals the process of transformation from deception to truth, from rebellion to restoration, from defeat to victory. Every believer will find themselves somewhere in this story, because renewal is not a one-time event; it's a continuous return to the Father's perspective.

In the next few minutes, we will look into the different ways one can reposition their mind for complete renewal.

1. Recognizing the Need to Renew the Mind

The younger son demanded his inheritance and pursued pleasure. He lived by the world's pattern: self-gratification, independence, and rebellion. His mindset was worldly, and worldly thinking always leads to destruction.

When famine came and his wealth was gone, he found himself feeding pigs, hungry, humiliated, and alone. The same is true today. The believer who lives apart from God's Word eventually reaches a spiritual famine. The first step to renewal is realizing that your current way of thinking isn't working.

Check the areas in your life where you desire victory and ask yourself, "How have I been thinking in this area", "Are these heaven's thoughts or earthly"? Victory begins when you admit, "This mindset is leading me nowhere."

2. Meditation and Reflection

Scripture says, *"When he came to himself."* (Luke 15:17). That is one of the most powerful phrases in all of Scripture. The prodigal son paused long enough to reflect on truth. Reflection creates space for revelation.

Many of us read and know the scriptures, but we only know them intellectually. This is because we seldom stop to reflect on what the scripture actually requires from us. This can only be achieved through meditation and reflection

In our busy, distracted generation, few people stop to think deeply about their lives. But victory requires self-examination. Like the prodigal, you must compare your current reality to God's promise. God's word already says a lot about you as a believer, and in all that it says... is your life compliant? Reflection is how the Holy Spirit reveals the misalignment. It is in stillness that truth breaks through deception.

3. Replacing Wrong Thoughts with Truth

The prodigal replaced his shame and pride with truth. He said, *"I will arise and go to my father."* (Luke 15:18). This reflects that he knew the truth about his father, that his father loved him dearly. He stopped saying, "I've failed," and started saying, "I will return." That's mind renewal in motion.

Many times, we find ourselves in a state that looks like defeat, and it is our own doing that got us at that point, but the word assures us of forgiveness. Transformation happens when your confession changes from defeat to faith. A modern believer might say, "I've messed up, but I'm not staying here. I am forgiven, and I'm returning to purpose." When truth replaces lies, your journey home begins.

4. Confession and Speaking God's Word

He rehearsed his confession before meeting his father. *"Father, I have sinned..."* (Luke 15:18-19). Confession is not just admission; it's alignment. When you confess truth, you reset your thoughts to agree with God's mercy.

Today, many believers remain bound because they won't speak truth. They hide behind silence instead of confessing God's promises. Victory comes when your words agree with His Word. Your mouth becomes the pen that rewrites your story.

5. Prayer and Seeking God's Mercy

His journey home was an act of prayer in motion. He didn't just wish for change; he walked toward it. Every step back to the Father was a declaration: "I trust Your grace." Prayer is not passive, it's pursuit.

When you pray with a renewed mind, you stop begging and start believing. You pray from sonship, not slavery. You walk by faith, knowing the Father runs to meet those who return.

6. Casting Down Mental Strongholds

The prodigal had to tear down pride, shame, and self-excuse. He didn't blame the famine or his friends; he took responsibility. (Luke 15:18). Victory in the mind requires honesty.

Strongholds fall when you stop defending lies and start embracing truth. Modern believers often justify bondage with excuses: "That's just how I am." But renewal says, "That's how I was, but not anymore." The renewed mind demolishes excuses and builds obedience.

7. Setting the Mind on Right Priorities

When the prodigal said, "I will arise and go to my father," his priorities shifted. He no longer pursued pleasure; he pursued presence. The renewed mind values relationship with God above all else.

In our generation, victory looks like choosing purpose over popularity, devotion over distraction, holiness over hype. Every time you prioritize intimacy with God over indulgence in the world, your mind is being renewed.

8. Receiving Guidance and Correction

When the father embraced him, forgave him, and clothed him, the son learned the nature of grace. Correction doesn't condemn, it restores. The Holy Spirit corrects not to shame us, but to shape us.

In a modern sense, this could be a believer convicted about sin. Instead of resisting, they yield, and healing flows. Correction is a gift that keeps the renewed mind humble and teachable.

9. Fellowship and Restoration

The father restored the son's position and identity. "Bring the best robe... put a ring on his hand." (Luke 15:22). Fellowship completes transformation. Isolation fuels deception, but community reinforces truth.

The renewed mind values accountability. Surround yourself with people who celebrate your return and protect your progress. Victory is sustained in the company of those who remind you who you are in Christ.

10. Worship and Gratitude

The father celebrated, *"Let us eat and be merry."* (Luke 15:23). Gratitude sealed the son's restoration. Worship is the language of the renewed mind; it is the language of victory. Thankfulness shifts focus from past failure to present grace.

Modern victory looks like praising God in the middle of process-thanking Him for what's already changing even before it's complete. Gratitude keeps your mind lifted above guilt. Worship keeps your perspective anchored in victory.

The prodigal son's renewal mirrors every believer's journey. He recognized his broken thinking, reflected, repented, and returned. His story teaches us that victory begins not when circumstances change, but when the mind does.

Renewing the mind is not about perfection; it's about progression. It's not about trying harder; it's about surrendering deeper. The mind that yields to God's truth will always live in victory, because the Spirit of Truth never fails.

The Father is still waiting for His sons and daughters to "come to themselves." When you return to right thinking, you return to right living. Victory through the mind is victory through surrender.

Let's Recap

Victory through the mind begins where surrender begins, in our thoughts. When the Word of God reshapes how we think, we stop conforming to the world and start walking in the will of God. The renewed mind learns to agree with truth even when feelings disagree.

The prodigal son's journey reminds us that transformation starts when we "come to ourselves," recognizing that our old ways of thinking lead to defeat. Renewal is not about perfection but alignment - letting the Spirit guide how we see, speak, and respond.

A renewed mind is one that thinks with faith, speaks with purpose, and lives with gratitude. It is the mind that no longer reacts to fear but responds to faith. Victory begins in that quiet place where your thoughts finally agree with God.

A Prayer for a Renewed Mind

Father, thank You for Your Word that renews and restores. Today I surrender my thoughts, emotions, and beliefs to You. Wash my mind with truth and silence every voice that does not come from You. Replace fear with faith, doubt with confidence, and confusion with clarity. Let the mind of Christ be formed in me.

Holy Spirit, teach me to think like Heaven, to see through the lens of grace, and to respond with wisdom. Just as the prodigal son returned to his father, I return to Your presence today. Renew my mind daily and let my life reflect Your victory. In Jesus' name, Amen.

Part Three

VICTORY IN THE PHYSICAL

STRATEGIES

S

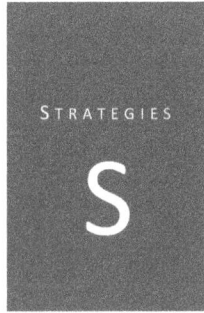

DAILY STRATEGIES

Principles give you the foundation for victory, but strategies teach you how to move in that victory. Principles tell you what God has already established; strategies show you how to cooperate with what He is doing. Victory is your inheritance, but strategy is your participation. Every breakthrough you will ever experience requires alignment - your steps aligning with God's instruction, your habits aligning with His wisdom, and your responses aligning with His leading. This section of the book is not theory; it is movement. These strategies are not formulas, but patterns taken from Scripture - ways God has led His people into triumph throughout every generation. Some strategies will stretch you, some will refine you, and others will reposition you. But each one carries the potential to shift your atmosphere, renew your perspective, and unlock what has been waiting on your obedience.

As you enter this part of the journey, remember: you are not learning how to fight for victory - you are learning how to walk out the victory Christ has already secured. Let these strategies become your rhythm, your posture, and your language. Apply them, practice them, embody them, and watch your life rise into the fullness of the triumph God designed you for.

STRATEGY

1

STRATEGIC SILENCE

Before the shout, before the trumpet blast, before the walls fell, God gave Israel a strict instruction: "You shall not shout or make any noise with your voice... until the day I say to you, 'Shout!'" (Joshua 6:10, NKJV). Strategic silence was part of the victory plan. Silence prevented premature celebration and protected them from speaking doubt or fear into the atmosphere. God knew that one wrong sentence could collapse morale before the walls even shook.

Spiritually, silence guards your destiny. Some victories require you to work quietly until God says, "Now speak." Not everyone is assigned to your victory, and some hearts carry envy, fear, or sabotage. Silence protects what God is building. Secondly, silence protects you from yourself - because many believers talk themselves out of breakthroughs by confessing fear, frustration, or unbelief. Heaven responds to faith - filled words, but hell responds to careless speech.

We live in an information age. People feel the need to announce every step of the way, to announce everything as and when it happens. As believers we seem to have been sucked into this way of doing things too. I have seen moments of vulnerability like a new business or even pregnancy being announced way before prayers have been made to God for heaven's direction. All your plans as a child of God have to be incubated in prayer first.

Share your goals with only those who cover you spiritually. Do not announce projects, relationships, ideas, or transitions prematurely. If God gives you an instruction, obey it silently. Work on your assignment without broadcasting it. Speak only when God says it's time to announce.

Strategic silence is not weakness - it is wisdom. It keeps your spirit focused, your faith protected, and your victory undisturbed. Some breakthroughs require you to move quietly until the trumpet sounds. When it's time to shout, God will make it clear. Until then, guard your mouth the same way Israel guarded their march - and the walls in front of you will fall in God's perfect timing.

STRATEGY

2

STRATEGIC STILLNESS

As Israel stood trapped between the Red Sea and Pharaoh's army, panic erupted. But Moses spoke a divine instruction that defied every instinct of self-preservation: *"Do not be afraid. Stand still, and see the salvation of the Lord... The Lord will fight for you, and you shall hold your peace."* (Exodus 14:13-14, NKJV). Stillness in the face of danger is not natural - it is spiritual. Strategic Stillness teaches us that when you have done all God asked and nothing seems to move, stillness becomes your weapon.

Spiritually, stillness is surrender. It is the posture that says, "God, I trust Your ability more than my fear." Stillness silences panic, fear, haste, and emotional decisions. It disarms the enemy by refusing to operate in anxiety and fear. Many breakthroughs are delayed not because God is slow, but because believers are too busy moving when God said "*be still.*" Stillness allows heaven to work without our interference.

Create moments of stillness daily - 5 minutes of no phone, no talking, no rushing. Sit before God and breathe deeply, acknowledging His presence. When confronted with a stressful situation, delay your response for 24 hours unless urgent. Practice spiritual stillness by loudly saying, "Lord, I trust You," instead of reacting. Build a habit of pausing for a while before decisions. Stillness is a strategy - schedule it intentionally.

Strategic Stillness reminds you that rest is not retreat - it is warfare. When you stop striving and stand still, God begins to fight. The sea in front of you will open, not because you pushed, but because you trusted. Stillness positions you for supernatural deliverance.

STRATEGY

3

STRATEGIC PRAISE

When Judah was surrounded by enemies on every side, Jehoshaphat did not sharpen weapons, strengthen walls, or strategize battle positions. Instead, *by the instruction of the Lord*, he positioned singers at the front of the army. Their only "weapon" was praise. And as they marched forward declaring, "Praise the Lord, for His mercy endures forever," God Himself set ambushes against the enemy. Confusion broke out, alliances collapsed, and the armies destroyed one another (2 Chronicles 20:21-24, NKJV). Strategic praise is not emotional singing - it's spiritual warfare that invites God to fight where human strength fails.

Spiritually, praise shifts the atmosphere. Hell cannot dwell where God is exalted, and darkness cannot occupy a room filled with worship. Praise breaks fear, interrupts anxiety, and brings the presence of God into a situation. When Paul and Silas were chained in the inner prison, they did not pray for escape - they praised. Heaven responded with an earthquake, every door opened, and every chain fell off (Acts 16:25-26, NKJV). Praise is a divine weapon the enemy hopes you never use.

Set a daily praise alarm - morning, noon, or evening. Build a playlist that exalts God's majesty, mercy, and goodness. Use your voice to exalt God's majesty, mercy, and goodness. Not every gospel song praises God, so choose songs that lift His name, not your emotions. Sing when you feel the pressure, when you get the bad news, when you're waiting for the job, or when the doctor gives the report. Sing when your home feels heavy. Praise on purpose. Worship in your car, in the shower, during your lunch break. Let praise go ahead of you like Jehoshaphat's singers.

Strategic praise may feel foolish when your house is threatened, your marriage is shaking, or your strength is failing - but heaven responds to praise in ways your hands never could. When you lead with worship, God follows with victory. Praise is the strategy that tells God, "I trust You more than the battle in front of me." And He has never failed the one who praises Him in the fire.

Paul and Silas were beaten, chained, and thrown into the inner prison - the darkest, foulest part of the jail. Every natural sign pointed toward defeat. Yet at midnight, the Bible says, "Paul and Silas were praying and singing hymns to God, and the prisoners were listening to them." (Acts 16:25, NKJV). Their praise shook the foundations of the prison, opened every door, and loosed every chain. This strategy us that praise is not a reaction to victory - it is a weapon that produces victory. Praise breaks what chains try to hold.

Spiritually, midnight praise is a declaration of faith. Praise confronts darkness by revealing that your trust is rooted in God, not circumstances. It invites heaven into the prison, into the disappointment, into the closed door. The enemy's assignment is always to suffocate your song, because he knows praise activates God's presence, and where God dwells, chains cannot remain. Your loudest praise must come in your darkest hour.

Choose a "midnight song" - a song that exalts God above your situation. Build a playlist titled "Chains Break Here." When fear rises, play it. When anxiety whispers, sing it. When discouragement hits, worship intentionally. Use praise as a scheduled spiritual weapon: praise during your commute, praise before difficult conversations, praise before bed. Let praise become your automatic response.

Strategic Praise teaches that worship is warfare. When you praise in pain, heaven responds with power. Your prison is never final when praise is present. Doors open. Chains break. Environments shift. Praise your way into the breakthrough.

STRATEGY

4

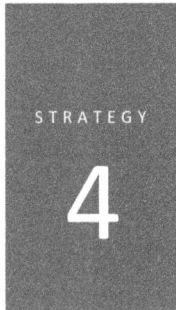

STRATEGIC FAITH

At a wedding where the wine had run out - an embarrassment for the hosts - Mary simply said, "*Whatever He says to you, do it.*" (John 2:5, NKJV). Jesus instructed the servants to fill waterpots with water. Ordinary action. No glow. No thunder. No sign. Yet as they obeyed the unusual command, water transformed into wine, and not ordinary wine - but the best wine of the feast (John 2:9-10, NKJV). Strategic faith teaches that miracles often hide behind ordinary instructions carried out with obedience.

Spiritually, God tests the heart through simple acts. Obedience creates divine access. Heaven values action rooted in trust more than emotion rooted in desperation. The servants did not understand the instruction, but they obeyed - and that obedience activated the supernatural. Many believers are waiting for a miracle while ignoring the instruction connected to the miracle. The greatest test of your faith is in how much you obey the simple instructions, simply because they are from God.

Do the simple things God has placed in front of you: fill out the application, read the chapter, give faithfully, show up on time, complete the task, repair the relationship, attend the meeting, or forgive someone. Miracles are often waiting behind routine faithfulness. Set a daily goal titled, "Do What He Says Today," and check it off once you've obeyed.

This strategy reminds us that water becomes wine when faith moves from just believing to being action. The ordinary becomes extraordinary when God is invited through simple obedience. Do what He says - no matter how basic - and watch God turn the ordinary into the miraculous.

STRATEGY

5

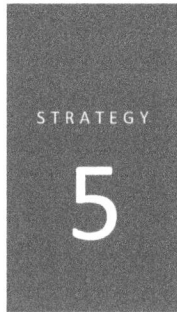

STRATEGIC INTERCESSION

Some of your victories will require you to stand in the gap for others - especially your family - even when they do not yet believe. God designed the family on purpose; it is one of Heaven's oldest assignments. Think of that young person in your home who dreams of university but has no clear path forward. You intercede. You lift their name before God. Suddenly doors open, wisdom increases, discipline grows, and they graduate.

They find work. They begin supporting the household. Those who once carried the weight of the family now have room to breathe, to rebuild, to help others. Your entire family rises because you prayed. What began as a personal burden becomes a generational breakthrough. This is why intercession matters. Moses understood it - Israel's victory became his victory. In the same way, when you pray for your family, Heaven writes your name into the testimony of their triumph.

Do not be too involved in sending money and doing other things but not involved praying for them. Raising your hands like Moses, on their behalf., raised hands symbolize surrender, dependence, and spiritual authority. Prayer shifts the unseen realm long before results appear in the natural. When you pray, heaven fights for you. When you stop, battles begin to turn against you. Strategic intercession teaches that consistency, support, and intercession keep your spiritual arms lifted in seasons of warfare.

Choose a prayer posture and stick to it daily - kneeling, standing, pacing, or hands lifted. Set a prayer schedule: morning, midday, and evening. Ask trusted believers to agree with you in prayer (your Aaron and Hur). Keep a journal of prayer requests and answered prayers. Before every meeting, interview, or assignment - pause and pray.

This strategy reminds you that the battle is never just physical. Your quiet prayer on the hill determines victory in the valley. When your arms grow tired, ask for support. Prayer is not preparation for the battle - it is the battle.

STRATEGIC OBEDIENCE

Israel reached Marah after days in the wilderness only to find water too bitter to drink. The people complained, but Moses cried out to God. The Lord showed him a tree and commanded him to throw it into the water. A simple act. A strange act. Yet the moment Moses obeyed, the waters were made sweet (Exodus 15:25, NKJV). Strategic Obedience reveals that breakthrough is never about the size of the instruction, but the size of the God who gives it.

Spiritually, obedience activates miracles. Heaven moves when earth yields. God uses small actions to unleash supernatural interventions because obedience realigns the believer with God's intention. What looks irrelevant or illogical becomes the gateway to healing, provision, and restoration. The enemy fights obedience because he knows one simple "yes" to God can reverse an entire season.

Pay attention to small nudges - apologize, give, fast, wake up earlier, call someone, apply for the opportunity, send the email, clean the room, sow the seed. These seemingly tiny steps can shift spiritual environments. Set a reminder daily to ask, "Lord, what is my obedience for today?" Then do exactly what He says, even if it feels insignificant.

Strategic Obedience teaches us that God does not need the spectacular - He needs your surrender. When you obey quickly, bitter places become sweet. What you cannot fix with effort, God transforms through obedience. Miracles often wait on the instruction you've been ignoring.

With the Red Sea before them and Pharaoh's army behind them, Israel stood trapped - at least in the natural. But God told Moses, *"Lift up your rod, and stretch out your hand over the sea and divide it."* (Exodus 14:16, NKJV). A wooden stick became the symbol of deliverance. What looked ordinary in Moses' hand became extraordinary in God's hand. Strategic Obedience reminds us that God often requires us to use what we already possess before He releases the miracle we are praying for.

Spiritually, the rod represents stewardship. God anoints what you use - not what you admire. Heaven partners with action. The sea did not part when Moses complained, when he prayed, or when the people panicked - it parted when Moses stretched out the rod. Sometimes the miracle is waiting at the end of an obedient action that feels too simple to matter.

Identify your "rod" - your skills, your job, your savings, your education, your influence, your phone, your opportunities. Use them intentionally. If you want open doors, refine your CV. If you want financial breakthrough, steward your budget. If you desire promotion, excel where you are. Work what God has already placed in your hand. Stretch it.

Strategic Obedience teaches us that God will use the simple to unlock the supernatural. You are not waiting for a miracle as much as the miracle is waiting for your stretch. Lift what you have. Use what you have. Trust the God who turns ordinary rods into pathways of deliverance.

Jesus spat on the ground, made mud, and anointed a blind man's eyes. He then instructed him to go wash in the pool of Siloam (John 9:6-7, NKJV). Nothing about this process made sense. It was unusual, uncomfortable, and unconventional - yet it produced undeniable healing. Strategic Obedience teaches us that God does not follow formulas. He uses unusual instructions because obedience reveals faith, and faith unlocks the miraculous.

Spiritually, unconventional obedience breaks religious rigidity. Many believers miss their miracle because they expect God to move in predictable ways. But God moves through obedience, not familiarity. Miracles often flow through uncomfortable instructions because they require humility, trust, and submission. What seems odd in the natural may be perfectly aligned in the spiritual.

Do the unusual thing God is prompting you to do: apply for the job you feel unqualified for, take the course that stretches you, apologize first, sow a seed that feels strange, pray at an unusual hour, or forgive someone without them asking. Create a journal titled "Unusual Instructions" and write down everything God impresses on your heart. Then obey it.

Strategic Obedience teaches that God is not limited to familiar methods. When you respond to unusual instructions with faith, heaven responds with unusual miracles. The blind see, the bound are freed, and the impossible becomes your testimony. Obey - even when it makes no sense.

STRATEGY

7

STRATEGIC CONSISTENCY

God instructed Israel to march around Jericho in silence - no climbing, no fighting, no shouting - just walking. For six days, they circled the massive walls once each day. On the seventh day, they walked seven times, blew the trumpets, lifted their voices, and God collapsed the walls Himself (Joshua 6:15–20, NKJV). The breakthrough did not come from force, noise, or strength. It came from obedience repeated consistently, even when it seemed pointless.

Spiritually, consistency trains your faith. Heaven responds to disciplined believers who do what God says even when results are invisible. Many victories are not delayed because of lack of power, but lack of persistence. Breakthrough often comes on the seventh lap, but too many believers quit on lap six. Consistency builds spiritual muscle and prepares your hands to handle the blessing when it arrives. Some miracles require endurance before manifestation.

Choose one spiritual discipline - prayer, scripture reading, fasting, generosity, or journaling - and commit to it daily for 30 days. Set reminders, block out time on your calendar, or create a routine you refuse to break. If your goal is career advancement, arrive early and leave late for a sustained consistent time. If it's fitness, commit to daily walking. If it's financial breakthrough, practice weekly budgeting. A drop of water seems useless - until it fills the bucket.

Strategic consistency is God's reminder that progress is often quiet before it is miraculous. Your obedience may look small, but heaven measures persistence, not speed. The walls wont even show the cracks, but keep marching, even if the walls look unmoved. Your seventh - day victory is hidden inside daily faithfulness. Do not stop on lap six.

STRATEGY

8

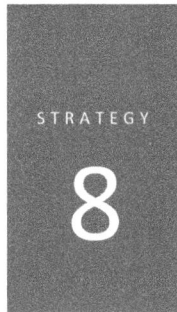

STRATEGIC TOOL

When David stepped onto the battlefield, all of Israel expected him to fight Goliath with the armor of a soldier. Saul tried to dress him in bronze, a sword, and a helmet - tools that made sense to men but did not fit David's calling. David removed the armor and chose a sling and five smooth stones (1 Samuel 17:38–40, NKJV). What looked childish - what looked insufficient - became the very instrument God used to bring down a giant. A Strategic tool reminds us that what God placed in your hand is enough when anointed by His power.

Spiritually, this strategy teaches us identity warfare. Heaven backs authenticity. God never asked you to be someone else or to fight battles with someone else's tools. The anointing flows where obedience and authenticity meet. When you embrace who God made you to be - your gifting, your personality, your skills, your calling - you fight with divine accuracy. Goliath wasn't defeated by skill alone, but by a man who refused to imitate, and instead used what God gave him.

Take inventory of your "tool": your abilities, your strengths, your experience, your spiritual gifts. Write them down. Some have a jawbone, some have a rod, others a jar of oil. Ask the Holy Spirit to show you where you've been wearing armor that doesn't belong to you - expectations, comparisons, or pressures from others, and the patterns of this world. Then commit to using what you have: start the business with the small idea; apply for the job even if your qualification seems "little"; use your phone to create content; learn the craft God has whispered to you. Your sling is enough.

This strategy reminds you that your victories will never come from imitation. They are birthed when you honor what God already placed in your hand. Giants fall when you dare to believe that your "small" carries supernatural accuracy. God has never required you to be big - He has only required you to be faithful with what you have.

STRATEGY

9

STRATEGIC ADJUSTMENTS

Most of us go through life without pausing to think, "where should I make adjustments". After fishing all night and catching nothing, the disciples were exhausted and discouraged. Jesus appeared on the shore and said, *"Cast the net on the right side of the boat, and you will find some."* (John 21:6, NKJV). A simple shift. The boat did not change. The waters did not change. The fishermen did not change. Only one thing changed - their obedience to adjust. And the Bible says they caught so many fish they could not drag the net into the boat. Strategic Adjustment teaches that small adjustments can produce supernatural results.

Spiritually, adjusting break stagnation. Sometimes you don't need a new job, new city, new relationship, or new assignment - you need a shift in posture, discipline, mindset, or obedience. God often positions abundance just a few steps away from where frustration lives. The blessing isn't far - it's just on the right side.

You cannot continue to do things the way you are used to doing them. Comfort strangles strategy. Your love for comfort should not exceed that of your victory. Ask God to show you areas of

179

adjustment in your life. Implement 1% daily improvements. Change your morning routine; adjust your prayer time; start reading 10 minutes a day; update your CV; reorganize your workspace; adjust your communication habits; optimize your sleep; limit social media; add one act of excellence daily. Small consistent shifts produce massive compounded impact.

This strategy reveals that your breakthrough may be one small adjustment away. You don't need to rebuild the boat - just cast the net differently. When you adjust as God instructs, you position yourself for abundance you did not even know was waiting.

STRATEGY

10

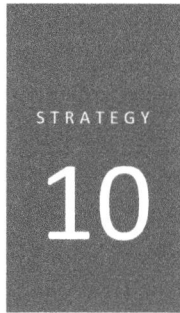

STRATEGIC DECLARATIONS

God brought Ezekiel into a valley filled with bones - dry, scattered, and lifeless. Then the Lord asked him a question that did not match the scene before him: *"Son of man, can these bones live?"* (Ezekiel 37:3, NKJV). Instead of asking Ezekiel to touch the bones, rearrange them, or gather them, God said, *"Prophesy to these bones, and say to them, 'O dry bones, hear the word of the Lord!'"* (v.4). As Ezekiel declared the word, bones found bone, tendons formed, flesh appeared, and breath entered them. What was dead became an exceedingly great army. Strategic Declaration reveals that heaven responds to what you speak, not what you see.

Spiritually, declarations align the natural with the supernatural. Words carry creative power because they originate from a creative God. Death and life truly are in the power of the tongue (Proverbs 18:21, NKJV). When you speak God's Word into dead situations - marriages, careers, finances, purpose, emotions - you release divine authority into the atmosphere. Hell attacks the believer's mouth because your words build what you believe.

Create a declaration list based on scripture. Speak it daily - morning and night. Declare healing even if symptoms remain. Declare provision even before the money arrives. Declare restoration even when the relationship looks buried. Replace complaints with prophecy. Set an alarm titled "Speak Life." Speak God's Word over your children, your mind, your home, and your work.

Strategic Declaration teaches that you cannot walk in victory with a defeated mouth. Speak what God says until what He says becomes what you see. The valley may be full of bones, but one declaration filled with faith can become the spark of resurrection.

When Israel once again cried out for water, God instructed Moses: *"Speak to the rock before their eyes, and it will yield its water."* (Numbers 20:8, NKJV). But Moses, frustrated by the people, struck the rock instead of speaking to it. Water still flowed, but Moses forfeited entry into the Promised Land. Strategic Declaration teaches us that in some seasons, God wants miracles produced not by force, but by words. When God says "speak," striking becomes disobedience.

Spiritually, speaking represents maturity. God trains believers to operate in authority through their words, not just their efforts. Some breakthroughs require you to decree, not perform. Force belongs to the flesh; declaration belongs to the Spirit. The enemy knows that if you learn to speak with authority, you will walk in dimensions he cannot stop - so he pushes you toward frustration and self-effort. But victory comes through alignment, not aggression.

Replace force with faith-filled speech. Instead of trying to fix everything yourself, declare the Word: speak healing, speak restoration, speak provision, speak peace. Wake up daily and read a scripture aloud. Begin your morning by declaring over your day: "I will not strike - I will speak." Keep a "decrees notebook" where you write what God says and speak it over your life consistently.

Strategic Declaration teaches us that some miracles are voice-activated. When you align your words with God's instruction, water flows from impossible places. Speak to the rock. Speak to the mountain. Speak to the dry place. Your victory is often waiting on your declaration.

11

STRATEGIC REDUCTION

Gideon began his assignment with 32,000 men, prepared to face the Midianites. But God reduced the number to 10,000, and then again to 300. Three hundred men armed with torches, clay jars, and trumpets (Judges 7:7, 16, NKJV). In the natural, this looked like guaranteed defeat. But in the spiritual, God was stripping away human confidence so that Israel would know that victory comes from the Lord. When the jars broke and the trumpets sounded, confusion fell upon the Midianite camp, and they turned on each other (Judges 7:19-22, NKJV). Strategic Reduction teaches us that less in your hands often means more in God's.

Spiritually, reduction is refinement. God removes what you don't need so that what remains can carry glory without distraction. Sometimes resources decrease, relationships end, opportunities close, or support disappears - not because you failed, but because God is preparing a victory that cannot be credited to human strength. Reduction clarifies, purifies, and intensifies your dependence on God.

185

Review your finances, commitments, and habits. Reduce intentionally: downgrade your car to free up financial peace, choose a smaller apartment to reduce pressure, cut unnecessary subscriptions, simplify your wardrobe, or create a boundary to protect your spiritual focus. Cut off some relationships and friends that cost you your peace. Reduction is not loss - it is strategic pruning. Sometimes the fastest way to grow is to remove what drains you.

Strategic Reduction reminds you that you never win because you have much - you win because God is with you. When God reduces your resources, He is strengthening your reliance on Him. What feels like subtraction is often preparation for supernatural multiplication. Less becomes a weapon when God is in the equation.

12

STRATEGIC DISCOMFORT

When the Shunammite woman's son died, Elisha did not stand at a distance and pray. He climbed onto the bed, stretched himself out on the child - mouth to mouth, eyes to eyes, hands to hands (2 Kings 4:34, NKJV). It was uncomfortable, unusual, and inconvenient. Yet it was this prophetic act that restored life. Strategic Discomfort teaches us that revival often flows through uncomfortable obedience. God will often ask you to do the thing that stretches you, challenges you, humbles you, and disrupts your comfort zone - because miracles rarely live where comfort lives.

Spiritually, discomfort is a catalyst. Heaven uses pressure to pull out purpose. Comfort breeds spiritual passivity, but discomfort sharpens discernment and deepens dependence. God grows you through stretching. Many believers pray for revival but resist the discomfort that births it. Revival requires closeness, sacrifice, and persistence. Discomfort breaks flesh so the Spirit can rule.

Wake up an hour earlier than normal for prayer. Stay late to complete the assignment with excellence. Drive your child to school instead of rushing them onto the school's transport. Take the extra course. Exercise even when tired. Decline the invitation that distracts you. Say no to the flesh even when it screams yes. Discomfort is a discipline – be intentional about it.

Strategic Discomfort reminds you that growth never happens in the soft places. God uses uncomfortable seasons and uncomfortable instructions to unlock unusual victories. Embrace the stretch - your miracle may be waiting on the other side of what feels inconvenient today.

STRATEGIC SURRENDER

A young boy handed over his small lunch - five loaves and two fish - to Jesus. What looked insignificant in human hands became supernatural in the Master's hands. Jesus blessed it, multiplied it, and fed thousands with baskets left over (John 6:11-13, NKJV). Strategic Surrender reveals that victory often begins not with what we keep, but with what we are willing to release.

Abraham understood this principle long before the crowd sat on that hillside. When strife broke out between his herdsmen and Lot's, Abraham surrendered his rights, his claim, and even the better land. He told Lot, *"Please separate from me; if you take the left, then I will go to the right; or if you go to the right, then I will go to the left."* (Genesis 13:9, NKJV). Lot chose the lush, fertile Jordan valley - the land that looked best. Abraham walked away with the less appealing portion, yet he walked away in victory. After Abraham surrendered, God immediately said, *"Lift your eyes... for all the land which you see I give to you and your descendants forever."* (Genesis 13:14-15, NKJV). Lot took what looked good; Abraham received what was God-given.

189

Spiritually, surrender is a divine exchange. When you give up what looks beneficial, God gives what is eternal. Surrender breaks the grip of fear and teaches the heart to depend on God's supernatural economy instead of human calculations. Heaven multiplies what you surrender but cannot bless what you cling to out of fear. Abraham surrendered land and gained a nation. The boy surrendered bread and fed a multitude. Surrender positions you for divine increase.

Identify areas where you are holding too tightly - relationships, opportunities, money, time, or control. Surrender intentionally: give even when it feels like you're losing, release the argument even when you're right, forgive even when you're wounded, sow the seed even when finances are tight. Schedule surrender by giving regularly, offering help, or dedicating time to God. Your "letting go" becomes God's "opening up."

Strategic Surrender teaches that God never subtracts - He multiplies what you trust Him with. When Abraham surrendered the land, God gave him the whole territory. When the boy surrendered his meal, God released a miracle. What you release determines what heaven can increase. Your victory is often wrapped inside your surrender.

STRATEGIC SERVICE

Jacob served Laban for fourteen years with strategic patience and excellence. His service was not accidental - it was purposeful. In Genesis 30:27, Laban confessed, *"I have learned by experience that the Lord has blessed me for your sake."* Jacob's service carried such weight that it transformed Laban's household. Strategic Service teaches us that serving faithfully where you are is often God's strategy to prepare you for where you are going.

Spiritually, service is sowing. When you serve, you activate principles of favor, elevation, and refinement. God tests character in service before He trusts you with leadership. Jacob served under manipulation, injustice, and unfair conditions - but God saw it, honored it, and multiplied him greatly. The fact that you serve those who are not faithfully rewarding you doesn't mean you need trade in your faithfulness for unfaithfulness. God is always watching you, and will reward you. Service is spiritual warfare against pride, impatience, and entitlement. God elevates servants before He elevates leaders.

Serve with excellence wherever God has placed you - home,

ministry, workplace, school. Arrive early. Stay consistent. Volunteer. Take initiative. Offer to help without being asked. Serve even when it feels unnoticed. Your service is a seed God will multiply.

Strategic Service reminds you that promotion does not come from man but from God. When you serve faithfully, heaven records it, and God rewards it. Jacob entered Laban's house empty - but through service, he left overflowing. Your service is your strategy.

STRATEGY

15

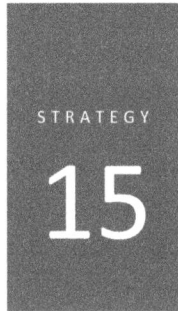

STRATEGIC HONOR

Honor is not flattery. It is not pleasing people. It is not pretending. Honor is the posture of a heart that recognizes the fingerprints of God upon a person, a place, or an instruction. Honor is Heaven's way of lifting a person without them lifting themselves. It is the currency of acceleration - doors open faster, favor flows easier, and opportunities multiply not because you pushed yourself forward, but because you honored rightly.

From the beginning, God has placed honor as a divine law: *"Honor your father and your mother, that it may be well with you..."* Honor births wellness. Honor births longevity. Honor carries blessing. When you honor those God has placed in your life - parents, leaders, elders, mentors, even colleagues - you align yourself with Heaven's flow of promotion. Dishonor closes doors quietly; honor opens them loudly.

Honor does not require agreement; it requires recognition. You may not agree with everything, but you can still honor the position God has entrusted to someone. David honored Saul even when Saul was driven by jealousy. David's honor preserved his destiny. His future was accelerated because his heart refused to dishonor even when he had every reason to. Some of your delays are not demonic - they are connected to dishonor in places God expected reverence.

Think of a workplace scenario. Two people may have the same skill, the same qualifications, even the same potential. One complains secretly, rolls their eyes, speaks carelessly about their senior, works half-heartedly, and wonders why promotion feels delayed. The other shows up on time, speaks with grace, refuses gossip, serves with excellence, and treats their senior with dignity even when they are difficult. Without striving, the second rises. They are noticed. They are trusted. They are accelerated. Honor did what talent could not.

Honor can shift a family. Imagine a young woman who decides to honor her aging parent by caring for them with patience, love, and generosity. Heaven sees it. Heaven records it. Heaven responds. Suddenly unexpected financial opportunities arise, her work becomes fruitful, and doors she didn't even knock on begin to open. Honor attracts God because it reflects God's heart.

This is the strategy: learn to honor in private and in public. Honor in speech and in action. Honor God, honor people, and honor the positions He has established even when the person holding the position is imperfect. Honor is not about them; it is about you - your posture, your heart, your alignment with God's order.

Honor may feel simple, but it is a force in the spirit. Where dishonor creates resistance, honor creates acceleration. When you choose honor, you choose a pathway of divine lifting that no man can stop.

STRATEGY

16

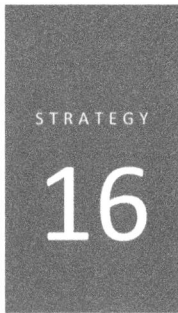

STRATEGIC GIVING

There are always opportunities to give to your victory. Cornelius was a devout man whose giving and prayers *"came up for a memorial before God."* (Acts 10:4, NKJV). His giving opened heaven, released angelic visitation, and extended salvation to his household. Similarly, the widow of Zarephath gave her last meal to Elijah - an act that made no natural sense during famine - yet her jar of flour and oil never ran dry (1 Kings 17:15-16, NKJV). Strategic Giving teaches us that giving is not loss - it is spiritual warfare that unlocks divine intervention.

Spiritually, giving breaks the power of scarcity, greed, and fear. Giving activates heaven's economy. It positions you under open heavens by demonstrating trust in God's provision. Giving is a seed that speaks in the spiritual realm long after it leaves your hand. The enemy fights giving because he knows generosity breaks cycles of lack and invites supernatural supply.

Sow intentionally - give faithfully, give offerings, bless someone in secret, support a ministry, buy groceries for a struggling family, or sponsor someone's education or transport. Make giving part of your monthly rhythm. Keep a giving journal to track seeds and testimonies. Give when it's easy and give when it costs you - both carry power.

Strategic Giving teaches us that your seed is a weapon. When you give, you speak into your future, fight spiritual battles, and open doors that prayer alone cannot open. Heaven responds to givers. Your generosity is a strategy for victory.

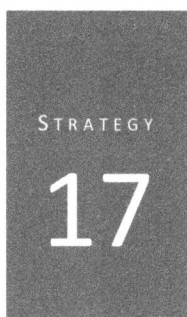

STRATEGY

17

STRATEGIC REST

After six days of creation, *"God rested on the seventh day from all His work"* (Genesis 2:2, NKJV). The Almighty - who neither slumbers nor faints - instituted rest as a holy rhythm. Jesus also told His disciples, *"Come aside by yourselves to a deserted place and rest a while."* (Mark 6:31, NKJV). Strategic Rest teaches us that rest is not laziness; it is obedience. Even God rested. Rest is holy, divine, commanded, and spiritual.

Spiritually, rest is restoration. When you rest, you reset spiritually, mentally, emotionally, and physically. Battles are lost when believers burn out, not when they run out. Rest heals the soul, sharpens perception, restores creativity, and strengthens spiritual authority. The enemy's agenda is constant exhaustion because a tired believer loses discernment. Rest is a spiritual strategy that recharges your ability to hear God clearly.

Schedule weekly rest. Turn your phone off for a set period. Take a monthly half-day retreat. Prioritize sleep. Replace one hour of scrolling with one hour of quiet or prayer. Observe a Sabbath rhythm - rest your mind, rest your body, rest your emotions. Rest intentionally, not accidentally.

Strategic Rest reminds you that rest is not optional - it is sacred. If God rested, so should you. Rest is worship. Rest is obedience. Rest is spiritual strength. Honor rest and watch your clarity, peace, and power multiply.

18

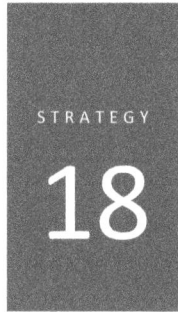

STRATEGIC FOCUS

While rebuilding Jerusalem's walls, Nehemiah faced relentless distraction - mockery, intimidation, and manipulation. His enemies invited him to a "meeting" four times, attempting to pull him away from the assignment. But Nehemiah responded with one of the most powerful declarations of focus in Scripture: *"I am doing a great work, so that I cannot come down."* (Nehemiah 6:3, NKJV). Strategic Focus teaches us that destiny is often lost, not through sin, but through distraction. Nehemiah refused to be derailed because he understood that availability is not the same as obedience.

When last did you disappear for the purposes of focusing on an assignment. Spiritually, focus is protection. Distraction is a spiritual attack designed to dilute power, creativity, and obedience. Hell does not need to defeat you if it can distract you. When you remain fixed on the assignment God has given you, you shut the door to spiritual manipulation. Focus is warfare - it preserves momentum and guards divine timing. The enemy often uses people, emotions, and unnecessary commitments to pull you "down" from the wall God called you to build.

Say "no" more often. Silence unnecessary notifications. Limit conversations that drain you. Block out daily focus hours and refuse to attend to anything else during that time. Create a "do not go down" list - things you will not entertain until your assignment is complete. You don't need a full calendar to be unavailable - your purpose is reason enough.

Strategic Focus reminds you that what you carry is great, and great work requires great boundaries. Nehemiah built a wall because he refused to come down. Stay on your wall. Protect your assignment. Heaven honors the focused builder.

19

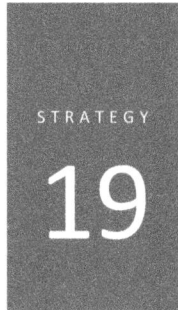

STRATEGIC RETREAT

Jesus often withdrew to lonely places to pray (Luke 5:16, NKJV). He retreated not out of fear, but out of spiritual intelligence. When pressure increased, He stepped away to refill. When decisions approached, He retreated to hear the Father. Similarly, Daniel requested time before giving the king an answer regarding the mysterious dream. That retreat into prayer birthed revelation (Daniel 2:16-19, NKJV). Strategic Retreat shows that stepping back is often the step forward heaven requires.

Spiritually, retreat restores clarity, sharpens discernment, and disconnects you from noise. It removes human interference so you can hear God clearly. Some battles are not lost because you are weak but because you are always in a crowd. Retreat is a weapon. Prayerful retreat is a spiritual recalibration that positions you to return with divine accuracy.

Schedule intentional retreats - even short ones. Take leave from work so you can fast and pray. Take a 24 - hour break from social media monthly. Spend one evening a week in quiet prayer instead of entertainment. Go for a prayer walk alone. Request time before making big decisions. If overwhelmed at work, take a brief pause to pray. Retreat before you respond. Retreat before you commit. Retreat before you collapse.

Strategic Retreat teaches us that victory does not always require movement - sometimes it requires stopping. You are strongest when you retreat into the presence of God and return with His strength. Silence before God is not escape; it is empowerment.

STRATEGY

20

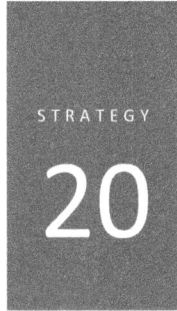

STRATEGIC BORROWING

A widow approached Elisha in desperation - her husband was dead, creditors were coming for her sons, and she had nothing left but a small jar of oil. Elisha instructed her to *"Go, borrow vessels from everywhere... do not gather just a few."* (2 Kings 4:3, NKJV). As long as vessels were available, the oil kept flowing. When the vessels stopped, the oil stopped (v.6). Strategic Borrowing teaches us that God's supply meets the level of your capacity. Sometimes you must gather from others what you lack so God can fill what you have.

Spiritually, borrowing speaks of humility, community, and capacity. God often increases you through what He has placed in others. Pride isolates; humility multiplies. Borrowing vessels means creating space - mentally, spiritually, physically - for God to pour out more. The oil never stopped because God ran out; it stopped because she ran out of capacity. Heaven always matches your preparation.

Borrow vessels through mentorship, volunteering, Job shadowing, learning, and asking for help. If you lack skill, borrow training. If you lack experience, borrow opportunity by serving. If you lack space, declutter. If you lack knowledge, read books, take courses, seek guidance. Increase your capacity intentionally. Write down: "A list of vessels you need to borrow in this season?" Then act on it.

Do you need an financial increase? learn how others manage finances, borrow that vessel. Are you aspiring for marriage? Attend marriage seminars, even as a single person, borrow that vessel. Strategic Borrowing reminds us that multiplication requires capacity. God cannot fill what you refuse to make room for. Humble yourself, gather vessels, and watch God pour until there is overflow. Your next level is tied to the capacity you create.

STRATEGIC POSITIONING

When famine gripped the land and everyone migrated to survive, Isaac remained where God told him to stay. He sowed seed in a drought - stricken land - an action that looked foolish and wasteful. Yet the Bible says, *"Then Isaac sowed in that land, and reaped in the same year a hundredfold; and the Lord blessed him."* (Genesis 26:12, NKJV). Strategic positioning teaches us that divine positioning rarely aligns with human logic. God blesses where He sends you - not where trends push you.

Spiritually, positioning means divine placement, and that placement may look like misplacement. When you obey God in seasons where everyone else is moving in the opposite direction, your obedience becomes a seed for supernatural harvest. Faith is tested most in famine - when the environment screams "don't sow," but God whispers "trust Me." Blessings multiply when you operate against fear and follow instruction instead of crowds.

Be intentional about doing the opposite of what fear tells you. Start the business when the market seems saturated. Take the course nobody else values. Stay when others run. Move when others stay. Volunteer where others avoid. Your "misplacement" may actually be your divine advantage.

Strategic Positioning teaches that God does not bless popular paths - He blesses obedient ones. What looks like the wrong place to man may be the right place for a miracle. When God says "sow here," the land - no matter how dry - will produce a hundredfold.

STRATEGY

22

STRATEGIC TESTIMONY

Your testimony is not simply a memory. It is a spiritual weapon. When the Bible says, *"They overcame him... by the word of their testimony,"* it is revealing a mystery: testimony is warfare. Testimony is victory spoken aloud. Testimony is a declaration that the God who delivered you before will deliver you again.

The enemy thrives in silence. He feeds on forgetfulness. When you stop remembering what God has done, your faith loses its fire. When you stop speaking of His goodness, your confidence begins to leak. Testimony is how you keep the flame alive. Testimony reminds your soul of what your spirit already knows. Testimony shuts the mouth of the accuser. Testimony builds an atmosphere where miracles are expected.

Think of my mother in-law who recovered from an illness doctors gave up on. She testifies. Every time she tells the story, faith rises in someone else's heart. Suddenly others believes healing is possible. Others begin to pray differently. Another home begins to declare life instead of fear. Her testimony becomes a seed that produces a harvest beyond her house.

Think of a young man who was drowned in addiction but encountered Jesus and was set free. When he speaks of his deliverance, he is not bragging - he is announcing that the chains he once wore have been broken forever. And every time he shares his story, someone who feels hopeless suddenly believes that freedom is possible for them too. His testimony becomes a lifeline for someone else's victory.

Testimony is also personal warfare. When you are going through a battle, speak of what God has done before. Remind yourself of every Red Sea He parted, every storm He calmed, every door He opened, every moment He rescued you. Your past victories become weapons against present intimidation. What God did becomes prophetic proof of what He will do again.

This is why the enemy wants you quiet. He fears your testimony because it exposes his defeat. He fears your testimony because it transfers courage. He fears your testimony because it magnifies God in the ears of those who are listening. When you testify, you are not just talking - you are building an altar with your words.

Strategic Testimony is the decision to speak of God's goodness intentionally, boldly, and consistently. Share your victories with your family, your friends, your church, and even your journal. Declare what God has done until the atmosphere around you shifts. **Celebrate the small victories.** Record the big ones. Tell your story even when you think it is insignificant - what seems small to you might be the key to someone else's breakthrough.

When you speak of what God has done, you step into the flow of what God is doing. Testimony is not a moment - it is a strategy. It is not nostalgia - it is spiritual warfare. It is not exaggeration - it is exaltation. By your testimony, you overcome, again and again.

Conclusion

All these strategies are not just information. They work, not because you are strong but because your God is. Victory has never depended on your ability, it has always depended on your alignment. When you posture yourself according to Heaven's patterns, the God who never loses begins to fight through you, for you, and around you. These strategies are the movements that activate the principles you learned, the steps that turn revelation into reality. As you apply them, expect atmospheres to shift, cycles to break, opportunities to open, and strength to rise. Victory is not a distant hope, it is the inevitable outcome for the believer who chooses to walk in God's way.

VICTORIOUS

V

LIVING FROM THE SEAT OF VICTOR

You are victorious. Victory has never been the reward of the qualified; it has always been the inheritance of the redeemed. From the first chapter of this book to the last, one truth has echoed consistently: God did not create you for defeat. There is nothing in your spiritual DNA that aligns with failure, fear, or bondage.

Everything about your new identity in Christ carries the fragrance of triumph. Every principle we explored, every strategy we uncovered, was Heaven's way of pulling back the curtain and showing you who you truly are in Him. Victory is not a destination you walk toward; it is a position you walk from. And as you stand at the end of this book, my prayer is that this revelation has not only informed you - it has transformed you.

We began with the foundations because every lasting structure rises from a sure base. Before any believer can walk in sustained victory, they must understand who they are, what Christ has done, and how Heaven has positioned them. Identity matters. Salvation matters. The

Word matters. The Name matters. The Blood matters. The Spirit matters. The mind matters. These are not optional components of the victorious life; they are the pillars that hold it up. Without them, no strategy will endure. And with them, no enemy can prevail. You may have read truths you have heard many times before, but revelation becomes transformation only when it settles into the heart and begins to shape the way you live. My hope is that as you turned each page, these truths settled deeper, strengthened firmer, and stirred faith within you that cannot be shaken.

But principles alone are not enough. Truth must become movement. Revelation must become expression. Identity must become action. It is not enough to know that you are victorious - you must learn how to walk as one who is victorious. That is why this book carried you beyond the foundations and ushered you into the realm of strategies.

The Christian life is not passive; it is purposeful. Victory is not accidental; it is intentional. God does not leave His people to figure out their battles through trial and error. He equips them with divine strategies - patterns of Heaven that, when embraced, turn ordinary believers into unstoppable warriors.

Throughout the strategies of victory, you encountered the many ways God leads His people into triumph. You learned that sometimes victory is found in silence, when God asks you to guard your mouth so the enemy cannot contaminate your atmosphere. At other times, victory is found in stillness, when the noise of life must bow to the voice of God. You discovered the power of consistency - the kind of daily discipline that creates spiritual momentum and strengthens every other strategy you apply.

You saw the beauty of obedience, not as a burden, but as the pathway through which God moves mightily. You learned the necessity of prayer, the courage of faith, the authenticity of the sling, and the humility of surrender. You walked through seasons of reduction, moments of declaration, rhythms of rest, and the protection of focus. You saw that victory sometimes requires retreat, sometimes requires bold service, sometimes requires radical giving, and sometimes requires divine repositioning or borrowing strength when your own seems insufficient.

None of these strategies were given to entertain your intellect; they were given to frame your lifestyle. Victory is not something you occasionally step into - it is something you continuously walk in. And walking requires rhythm. Every strategy in this book was designed to give you rhythm. Some rhythms are quiet, some are loud. Some are fast, some are slow. Some stretch you, some stabilize you. Some correct you, some empower you. But all of them lead you deeper into the victorious life Christ purchased for you.

If there is one truth I want to leave you with, it is this: victory is not fragile. It does not shatter when life gets hard. It does not disappear when the enemy tries to intimidate you. It does not dissolve under pressure or fade during warfare. Victory is robust. Victory is anchored. Victory is blood-sealed, Spirit-empowered, and Christ-centered. You may feel shaken, but your victory never is. You may feel stretched, but your victory never weakens. The battles you face do not redefine you; they reveal you. They uncover the strength God planted within you, the authority He placed upon you, and the strategies He entrusted to you.

As you close this book, understand that you are not closing the revelations it contains. You are stepping into a life where these truths must now become your daily breath. The world you return to, the responsibilities that await you, the battles you may have paused while reading - none of them diminish what God has done in you through these pages. In fact, they now become the stage upon which you will manifest the victory you have learned.

Do not return to life as if nothing has changed. Let your posture change. Let your prayers change. Let your silence be strategic, your obedience be immediate, your declarations be bold, and your rest be holy. Let your consistency speak louder than your emotions. Let your surrender open doors your strength never could. Let your faith take aim like David's sling. Let your life announce - without apology - that you know who you are and whose you are.

Victory is not just personal; it is generational. Every stronghold you defeat becomes freedom for those who come after you. Every strategy you apply becomes a pathway for someone else. Every breakthrough you walk in becomes a testimony of God's faithfulness to those who watch your life. You are not just fighting for yourself; you are fighting for the destiny of your family, the integrity of your assignment, and the expansion of God's Kingdom through you. Heaven is invested in your victory because your victory magnifies Christ.

As you go forward, walk with this assurance: nothing in your life is random. Nothing you face is wasted. God is too intentional, too precise, too loving, and too wise to allow anything into your life that cannot be used for your good and His glory. Every battle is an invitation to apply what you have learned. Every challenge is an opportunity to prove what you believe. Every season - whether restful or restless - is a moment to demonstrate the strategies of Heaven.

So now I send you forth - not as a survivor of life's storms, but as a conqueror marked by grace. Not as one who is trying to find victory, but as one who already carries it. Not as a believer who merely understands principles, but as a warrior who lives by strategy. Not as a child of circumstance, but as a child of God. You have been taught, equipped, strengthened, and awakened. You have been reminded of who you are, empowered to walk boldly, and given everything you need to live triumphantly.

Walk in the truth that victory is not your goal - it is your identity. Walk as one who knows that Heaven's backing is greater than Hell's attacks. Walk with confidence in the God who never loses. Walk with faith in the Christ who reigns. Walk with dependence on the Spirit who empowers. And as you walk, may your life become the loudest declaration of all:

Jesus has won, and because He has won, I will never live defeated.

This is your life now.
This is your inheritance.
This is your victory.

A LETTER FROM THE AUTHOR

Thank you for purchasing this book and for taking the time to read it. Your willingness to journey through these pages means more to me than you know. If this book has spoken to you, strengthened you, or stirred something within your spirit, I would truly love to hear from you.

Your voice matters. Your experience matters. Your reflections carry weight - not only for me as I grow in my assignment, but also for the next reader who may discover this book because you chose to share your encounter with it.

If you feel led, please take a moment to leave a review on TikTok, Amazon, Goodreads, or Facebook. The process is simple:

Use the hashtag: #HeavenlyStrategies

Every review - long or short - is a seed. It helps this message reach further, shine brighter, and impact lives beyond what I could ever do alone.

And if you don't have access to any of these platforms, I still want to hear from you. You matter to me.
Please feel free to reach out at: info@verseconnect.co.za

Thank you for reading. Thank you for sharing. Thank you for being part of this journey of victory.

With honor and gratitude,

Innocent B. Maluka

Ministry

M

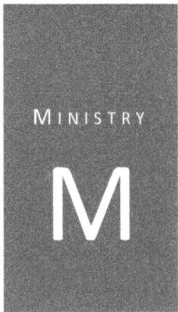

MINISTRY INVOLVEMENT

As a child of God, I count it both a blessing and a sacred trust to serve through the following ministries:

Verse Connect

Verse Connect is an interdenominational Bible study ministry dedicated to making Scripture practical, relatable, and alive for today's generation. Through creative weekly topical Bible studies, and monthly book-based Bible discussions, Verse Connect bridges the timeless truth of Scripture with the reality of modern life.

Our mission is simple, to help believers attain victory and remain victorious through God's Word. We aim to teach in a way that is clear, engaging, and deeply transformative.

B&M Relationship Consulting

B&M Relationship Consulting is a faith-based relationship ministry committed to building, strengthening, and restoring marriages and relationships upon biblical foundations. We believe that every relationship can be renewed through the Word of God.

B&M goes beyond offering advice, it's a ministry of transformation, helping couples rediscover love, honor, and divine purpose in their union. Our desire is to guide partners toward relationships that reflect Christ's love, relationships that are both God-honoring and joy-filled.

Contact: Info@verseconnect.co.za

The End

www.ingramcontent.com/pod-product-compliance
Lightning Source LLC
Chambersburg PA
CBHW051724040426
42447CB00008B/962